FLOWERS & FANTASIES
IN THE
GARDEN

A guide for gardeners and stories for romantics

Jeannette Hill McCarty

Illustrations by Craig Tyler

The McCormack Publishing Company
Riverside, California

First Edition

Library of Congress Catalog Card Number: 92-63257

FLOWERS & FANTASIES IN THE GARDEN
A guide for gardeners and stories for romantics

By Jeannette Hill McCarty

1. Gardening   2. Garden Fantasies   1. McCarty, Jeannette Hill
ISBN 0-9635434-0-7
Printed in the United States of America

Book Design by Tom Mossman
Cover Design by Barbara Davis

Distributed in the United States by Hilltop Enterprises
1075 Lagunita Road
Pasadena, California 91105-2223

Dedicated to
my old gardening friend
Don Goodrich,
who introduced me to
the delights and perils of gardening,
and to the
Wise Old Owl in the Ginkgo Tree.

ACKNOWLEDGEMENTS

I am most grateful to many for sharing with me their enthusiasm and sage advice. A few are: Paul Frame, author and illustrator; Thomas A. Chandler, founder of Chandler School; Mary Helen Roth, who loves my garden as much as I do; Bill Finucane; Ada Gates; Jim Shea; John, my husband, who ate many late dinners, and most of all Tom Mossman, graphic designer.

CONTENTS

Gardening

Illustrations

28 Mini Stories

Flowers

Flowers

PREFACE

Most gardening books are a bore, but they are as necessary as breathing in and breathing out. I have endeavored to enliven this book by sprinkling it with short stories, anecdotes, fantasies, and quotes. Knowledge and enthusiasm are two important ingredients for a successful gardener, and I hope this book imparts both to those who are interested in horticulture.

The first ten chapters are briefly devoted to the essentials of gardening. Four compact chapters discuss bulbs, ferns, ground covers, and succulents. These are followed by 104 mini-chapters on the most popular flowers found in gardens. Complete planting and care is given for each one.

Climate zones have been simplified into mild, hot, and cold. Arboretums and local nurserymen know best what plants are successfully grown in a particular area.

Jeannette Hill McCarty

"There is no subject so old that something new cannot be said about it."

Dostoevski

1

GARDENING APPAREL

The well-dressed horticulturist never wears Guccis when working in the garden. The following is the proper attire for those who are discriminating.

A Hat with a Wide Brim

An Old Shirt
The older the better. Juices from many plants make permanent stains.

Blue Jeans or Shorts
Whichever one is best for the current weather conditions.

High Rubber Boots
Wear these in the winter. In the summer, I like to slosh around in bare feet or sandals.

Gloves
Optional. Personally, I can't cope with them unless I am pruning roses.

"So long as we are dirty,

we are pure."

Charles Dudley Warner,

"My Summer in a

Garden", 1870

2

BARE NECESSITIES

 Gardening had its humble beginnings 10,000 years ago when the Ice Age ended and Homo Sapiens came out of their caves to organize Garden Clubs and to invent a vast number of tools. Today there are about as many implements for gardening as there are remedies for the common cold, but the following ones are sufficient for the average gardener.

"Neither a borrower

nor a lender be;

For loan oft loses

both itself and friend."

Shakespeare

Clippers
> Always have them with you. They are a gardener's best friend.

Two Trowels
> One is to use when the other one can't be found. They should have sturdy shanks so they won't break easily.

Hoses
> Have a hose attached to every faucet. Don't buy cheap ones which kink and stop the flow of water, but not the flow of "bleeped" words.

Also

> A shovel, rake, hoe, spade, spading fork, shears, wheelbarrow, cultivator, watering can, measuring spoons for insecticides and fertilizers, a low stool to sit on while weeding, and a large comfortable chair to fall into after hours in the garden.

"Have a place for

everything and keep

the thing somewhere else.

This is not advice,

it is merely custom."

Mark Twain

Things My Mother Never Told Me

- Keep all small tools in a basket or a bucket, and paint their handles a bright red for easy spotting.
- Clean tools after each use by wiping them with a slightly oiled rag.
- Keep all gardening equipment in one central place. Hang the larger tools on a wall.

3

SOIL AND SEX

This is probably the most important chapter in the book. There is no sex involved, but I have included it in the title to get your attention and trap you into reading it. Please forgive my chicanery, but good soil is vital for a successful garden. Mother Nature and all the gods on Mt. Olympus can be of no help if the soil is not good. Fortunately, for the lazy gardener, there are many different planting and potting mixes. Many are pre-mixed and ready to use. Gardening is a waste of time if the soil is poor.

"How cunningly nature hides every wrinkle of her inconceivable antiquity under roses and violets and morning dew!"

Ralph Waldo Emerson

A Mini-Course on Soil

There are three basic types of soil: Sandy, Clay, and Well-Balanced
- In sandy soil, water drains quickly and washes away nutrients.
- Clay soil is heavy and compact and water does not drain quickly.
- Well-balanced soil is composed of 1 part sand, 1 part clay, and 1 part soil amendment.

There are two types of soil amendments: Organic and Mineral
- The organic amendments are humus, compost and others.
  Humus is the natural decomposition of matter which comes mainly from forests and peat bogs.
  Compost is the general term used for decomposed vegetable matter such as grass clippings, leaves, and scraps from the kitchen.
  Others are manure, leaf mold, sphagnum moss, ground bark, sawdust, hay, straw, seaweed, peanut shells, etc.
- Mineral amendments are pumice, perlite, and vermiculite.
  Pumice and **perlite** are a kind of volcanic glass. They are often used as a substitute for sand in soil mixes to make the soil lighter and to give it better drainage.
  Vermiculite is a sponge-like mineral often used as a substitute for leaf mold or compost in soil mixes.

4

SOIL AND SEX

Some facts about alkalinity and acidity in soil
- Soil with too much alkaline or too much acid is not good for most plants.
- A soil is alkaline when it is high in lime, salts, and other minerals. This often occurs in areas where there is little rain. It is neutralized by deep watering which leaches these minerals, by adding peat moss or ground bark, or by using an acid-type fertilizer.
- A soil becomes acid when minerals are leached from the soil. This usually happens in areas where there is much rain. It is neutralized by adding lime, manure, or straw. Azaleas, camellias, and rhododendrons thrive in acid soil.

A simple test for alkalinity or acidity in a soil
- Place some moist dirt from the garden in the middle of a piece of litmus paper. If the soil is mostly acid, the paper will turn red. If it is mostly alkaline, the paper will remain blue. Samples of soil can also be sent to most State Universities to be tested.

The pH scale
- The acidity and alkalinity of soils is measured in terms of the pH scale, which is from 1 to 14. A pH of 7.0 is neutral. Any reading below this is acid and any reading above it is alkaline. Now impress your friends with all your knowledge!

"Not every soil

can bear all things."

Virgil

"An expert is one who claims he knows more and more about less and less."
Nicholas Murray Butler

4

FERTILIZERS FOR ANEMIC PLANTS

 ertilizer is the magic elixir that helps turn scrawny plants into healthy, beautiful ones. In the olden days all fertilizers were organic. Along with the development of rockets, computers, cloning, and the Super Bowl came the development of chemical fertilizers. Both supplements are used today and both are equally effective.

There are three primary elements in fertilizers: Nitrogen, Phosphorus, and Potassium (NPK).
- Nitrogen (N) stimulates the growth of young shoots and leaves, and gives leaves a rich, green color.
- Phosphorus (P) helps the growth of good root systems. When planting or transplanting, mix some with the soil at the bottom of the hole.
- Potassium (K) encourages the development of flower buds and produces sturdy stalks and stems.

"The greater our knowledge increases, the greater our ignorance unfolds."

John F. Kennedy

Percentages of these elements are listed in numbers on packages of fertilizers. Nitrogen is always first, phosphorus is always second, and potassium is always third. Therefore, 8-12-4 means 8% N, 12% P, and 4% K.

The different types of fertilizers are: All Purpose Fertilizers, Fertilizers for Specific Plants, and Fertilizers for Specific Needs.
- There are many different kinds of all purpose fertilizers. Each has varying amounts of NPK in its formula.
- Roses, azaleas, and citrus are just a few of the many plants that have specific fertilizers formulated for them.
- Fertilizers for specific needs usually have a high percentage of one or two elements. Superphosphate (0-20-0) is used to develop good root systems. A fertilizer low in nitrogen and high in phosphorus and potassium (2-10-10) is used to produce large blooms. Use this when a plant is setting its buds.

FERTILIZERS FOR ANEMIC PLANTS

Most gardeners have a favorite fertilizer whose honor they vehemently defend. One organic gardening friend has a truck load of manure dumped in her garden every spring. Another one uses a fish emulsion because nutrients are released slowly. Most use an all purpose fertilizer with a balanced formula. Many nurseries use a 20-20-20 formula.

When to Fertilize
- Some gardeners fertilize in the spring when new growth appears and once again in three months.
- Some fertilize once a month, and others every two weeks.
- Many plants such as roses, azaleas, camellias, fuchsias, and begonias require special feeding schedules.
- If you are confused, simply follow the instructions on the package or bag of fertilizer.

Things My Mother Never Told Me
- Most plants have a period of dormancy. Do not feed at this time.
- Water a plant before it is fertilized - unless the soil is already wet. This prevents root burn.
- Set up a regular schedule for fertilizing.
- Have a separate calendar for garden activities, and mark down every time you fertilize. Don't rely on your memory.

5

TO WATER OR NOT TO WATER, THAT IS THE QUESTION

 I t is a very wise man who knows just when and how much to water. There are no set rules. No pat formulas. Many factors are involved such as the soil, the season, the temperature, the wind, the humidity, and the needs of each plant. All of these are variable. However, there is one rule to follow: Do not sprinkle lightly every day or so, and do not give your garden frequent heavy soakings. Water less frequently and water thoroughly.

There are four basic ways to water:
Overhead Sprinkling, Irrigation, Soaking, and Drip Irrigation
- Overhead sprinkling keeps leaves clean and discourages many pests. However, plants that are subject to mildew, such as roses and zinnias, should not be watered by this method.
- Irrigation is used in cutting beds and in vegetable gardens. Furrows are made between the rows of plants and are flooded.
- Soaking is a thorough way of watering large plants, shrubs, and trees. Dig circular wells around them to concentrate the water. An attachment called a "bubbler" can be put on hoses for easy soaking of flower beds.
- Drip irrigation has become popular in areas where conservation of water is a big factor. A system of small tubes slowly feeds water to plants and pots. Water consumption can be cut almost in half by this method.

"Rain is good for vegetables and for the animals who eat those vegetables - and for the animals who eat those animals!"

Samuel Johnson

TO WATER OR NOT TO WATER, THAT IS THE QUESTION

- Do not water overhead in the middle of a hot day as plants might get scorched.
- On very hot days, briefly turn on sprinklers for a short time in the early evening to revive plants, but do not consider this as watering them.
- Save rainwater in an old-fashioned rain barrel - if you can find one - or use a large metal container. Large plastic ones will spring a leak. Rain is beneficial to plants because it helps to leach built up salts that have accumulated in the soil.
- Never leave water in a saucer or tray under a plant. If a plant from a florist or a nursery has tin foil around it, remove it immediately to prevent root rot.

"Although it rain,

cast not away

the watering pot."

Malay Proverb

Things My Mother Never Told Me
- It's time to water if a trowel, a sharp stick, or a finger cannot easily be pushed into the soil for more than three inches.
- The best time to water is early in the morning. This helps prevent water mold, fungus, and mildew.
- If a clay pot is lined with plastic, it retains moisture longer. Be sure there is good drainage.

6

INSECTS AND PESTS
or "Quick, Henry, the Flit!"

Insects and pests of all kinds, shapes, and descriptions lurk in every garden. They are found beneath, beside, under, and on anything living or dead. Many wear disguises that are so fantastic they are extremely difficult to find, and some are so miniscule they are invisible - such as the famous no-see-um bugs. There are pests that suck, chew, burrow, bore, cut, and chomp. Plants can be completely devoured by their ravenous appetites.

Snails and slugs are the most common and plentiful garden villains from Puyallup to Pensacola. They arrive in massive droves in the spring to hold nightly orgies of feasting on tender new shoots. They chomp and chew and pas de deux! Some gardeners say Society Garlic (Tulbaghia violacea) planted near flowers will keep away snails. In my garden, snails even eat the garlic plant! A shallow pan filled with beer, or a grapefruit cut in half are supposed to attract snails for easy killing. Snail bait is still the best way of getting rid of these pests, and there are many good ones available. Change brands occasionally as snails become immune to one kind after a period of time. For the adventurous gardener, there is always snail hunting in the middle of the night or in the early morning while the dew is still on the ground. Hundreds of snails can be wiped out in an hour.

Aphids are another common pest. They are tiny green, black, lavender, or yellow insects that suck, and they cause great damage. Hosing them off with a strong spray of water often discourages them from returning. Ladybugs love them. Onions, garlic, and parsley grown near a plant are supposed to keep away aphids. Good luck!

"God in his wisdom

made the fly and then

forgot to tell us why."

Ogden Nash

INSECTS AND PESTS

Some other sucking insects are spider mites, whiteflies, mealybugs, scale, thrips, and spittle bugs. A few chewing pests are beetles, caterpillars, earwigs, grasshoppers, and weevils. Cutworms, grubs, soil mealybugs, and wireworms are some of the insects that live in the soil and eat the roots of plants.

Most all garden pests can be controlled by spraying with either an organic or chemical spray. Two excellent organic pesticides are rotenone and pyrethrum. Dipel, Malathion, and Sevin are brand names of some of the widely used chemical insecticides. Your nurseryman will tell you which one is best for your needs.

There are also systemic insecticides. Granules can be sprinkled in the soil or plants can be sprayed. The chemicals in both methods are absorbed by plants. Only sucking insects are killed by this method.

Many large pests also decimate gardens. A few are deer, gophers, moles, rabbits, mice, birds, and pets. These are controlled by various methods such as setting traps and placing wire screening under and around plants.

Things My Mother Never Told Me
- Remove all debris, dead leaves, and weeds from a garden. These are natural hiding places for pests. A clean garden will have many fewer problems than an untidy one. Mulch with redwood shavings to control the weeds.
- Use insecticides only when necessary, and read the instructions carefully. Do not leave them in reach of small children.
- Mix one teaspoon of a non-detergent, liquid soap such as Ivory Soap with a gallon of water for a non-toxic pesticide.

INSECTS AND PESTS

All Purpose South of the Border Insect Spray
for the 100% Organic Gardener

Dedicated organic gardeners never use chemical pesticides. They rely mostly on faith and prayer. I am in total awe of them. However, I believe most pesticides, if carefully used, will not do irreparable harm to the environment, and they will vastly improve it by getting rid of some very destructive pests.

The following make-it-yourself spray is completely organic and can be used without any qualms or guilty feelings by even the most ardent ecologist.

Grind
- 4 hot peppers
- 4 large onions
- 2 whole garlic bulbs
- 3 crumbled cigarettes (remove the paper)

Put the above ingredients in a bowl of water. Cover bowl with aluminum foil and let sit overnight. Strain ingredients through a fine sieve and add enough water to make one gallon. Spray plants with the above concoction several times daily for two or three days. If this doesn't get rid of insects, it should at least give them Montezuma's Revenge!

7

PLANT DISEASES
Now for the bad news

There are approximately 100,000 diseases that strike plants. They are usually caused by a virus, bacteria, or fungus. It is easier to prevent these diseases than it is to cure them. One of the best preventative measures against disease in a garden is a clean garden. Plants can also be sprayed with a fungicide before symptoms appear.

"Diseased nature

oftentimes breaks forth

in strange eruptions."

Shakespeare

A few of the most common diseases are listed below. There are many other chemicals than the ones suggested that will control the various diseases. Ask your nurseryman which one is best for you.

Botrytis Blight or Gray Mold Blight: Splotches on plants that later turn into gray mold.
> Common during cool, damp, summer weather. Remove infected parts and spray with zineb or a copper spray.

Damping Off: Attacks seeds and seedlings.
> Seeds do not sprout and seedlings topple over because their tiny stems wither. Dust seeds with a fungicide before sowing and keep them barely moist.

Fire Blight: Leaves and stems look like they were burned by fire.
> Insects spread this disease. During the blooming season, spray every four or five days with Fixed Copper.

Gall: Swollen or abnormal growth.
> Caused by insects feeding on plant tissue, or an infected wound. Small plants should be destroyed. Prune infected branches of woody plants and remove them from the garden.

Leaf Spot: Spots on leaves become dead.
> Attacks during cool, wet weather. Dust with sulphur or spray with zineb.

PLANT DISEASES

Powdery Mildew: A light mealy coating forms on leaves and stems.
Plants become deformed or dwarfed. Often occurs when plants are crowded and have poor air circulation. Also in late summer when the nights are cool and the days are still warm. Spray both sides of leaves with benomyl or sulphur. Repeat in a week.

Rust: Rusty spores form on the underside of leaves.
Spray with sulphur or zineb. Remove infected plants before these spores burst. Snapdragons are prone to this disease.

Shot Hole: Small round spots on leaves which often drop out and produce a hole.
Spray with zineb.

Wilt: Leaves droop, become yellow and die.
A systemic disease which usually attacks through the roots. Soil can be fumigated for shallow rooted plants, but this is not too successful with deep rooted ones.

"Most men die of

their remedies,

not of their diseases."

Molière

Things My Mother Never Told Me

- Before reusing flower pots, toss out the old soil. Scrub and soak pots in a tub filled with water that has had a strong dose of Clorox added to it. This helps prevent the recurrence of any disease the former occupants might have had.
- After pruning or cutting diseased plants, disinfect all tools with a solution of 70% denatured alcohol, or a solution of a household bleach.

8

BRIEFLY ABOUT LANDSCAPING

Landscaping is for the professionals. Do not make the mistake of planning a garden yourself or asking a well-meaning, but untrained, friend to do it for you. Work with qualified landscape architects. Tell them what your basic needs are as well as your favorite plants and colors. They will draw up a plan and will either oversee the work or recommend someone else to do it.

"A bad beginning

makes a bad ending."

Euripides

A less expensive way to plan a garden is through a nursery. Many have knowledgeable men and women who will give excellent gardening advice for an hourly fee. Shop around first before you settle on one person or one nursery. Get at least two or three different plans and bids, and beware of the self-proclaimed expert.

"Trust ivrybody - but cut th' ca-ards."
Finley Peter Dunne

9

STATUES, FOUNTAINS, GAZEBOS
and other Bric-a-Brac

The Wise Old Owl in the Ginkgo Tree knows that many beautiful gardens are ruined by the addition of phony, plaster statues of Greek gods and goddesses, nude females, ducks, pink flamingos, frogs, turtles, snails, storks, and ad infinitum. I wish I could dump in the ocean everything plaster and plastic, but then the ecologists would rightfully chastise me.

Europe is famous for its ancient castles and palaces with acres of lawns filled with magnificent statuary and fountains. Many of these gardens are so beautiful they are almost mythical, but who has a garden the size of a feudal estate!

Today, when a statue is added to a garden, it should be done with great caution. It is difficult and expensive to find lead and marble ones that are the right size for the modern garden. Small, stone, French statues and urns are plentiful, but unless your house is in the French style, these often look out of place.

Fountains can be a pleasant addition to almost any garden. The sound of splashing water is very soothing and relaxing, and in hot climates they help one survive. Fountains should never overpower a garden. They should be in perfect balance with the garden and the house.

Gazebos have had more than their share of popularity over the years, and deservedly so. There is nothing more charming than a beautifully designed one that is properly placed in a large garden, and there is nothing worse than one stuffed into a small garden.

Sundials and birdbaths are also often found in gardens. If the right spot for them can be found, and if they are not made out of plaster or plastic, they can be attractive.

Nothing is more beautiful and mystifying than nature itself. Don't clutter it with unnecessary things.

10

A SHORT DISSERTATION ON BULBS

 Some of the most glamorous flowers in the garden trace their heritage to an ugly bulb. A bulb is a swollen or thickened part of a stem. A tuberous root is a swollen part of a root. Bulbs, corms, rhizomes, tubers, and tuberous roots are all loosely classified as bulbs because they all provide nourishment to a new growth cycle after a dormant period. A few examples of each classification follows:

True Bulbs
> Dutch Iris, hyacinths, narcissus, lilies, and tulips.

Corms
> Crocus, freesias, and gladiolus.

Rhizomes
> Crested, bearded, and beardless Iris. Also calla lilies.

Tubers
> Ranunculus, tuberous begonias, and cyclamen.

Tuberous Roots
> Cannas, dahlias, and clivias.

Planting
- All bulbs like a soil that is on the porous side and one that has good drainage.
- Mix a small amount of bonemeal with the dirt at the bottom of the planting hole.
- A rule of thumb is to plant bulbs at a depth approximately three times their greatest diameter. In sandy soils plant them a little deeper. In heavy soils sprinkle a layer of sand at the bottom of the hole, and do not plant them so deep.

Care
- Bulbs like lots of water when they are growing.

A SHORT DISSERTATION
ON BULBS

- Do not cut off the stems and leaves before they have yellowed and died. They make the food that is stored in the bulb for next year's growth. After a plant has bloomed, the leaves can be pulled together, folded over, and tied with a rubber band until they turn yellow. Then cut them off with a sharp knife or clippers.
- Some gardeners dig up their bulbs and store them until they are to be planted again the following year. Others let them remain in the ground.

Storing

- Before storing bulbs, let them dry out for about a week in a dark, well ventilated place.
- When bulbs are dry, carefully remove excess dirt and dust them with a fungicide powder to help prevent rot.
- Store in a dark, cool room. The basement is usually a good place.
- Rodents, snails, and slugs will nibble bulbs if they can reach them.
- Do not let water or moisture get on bulbs as this could cause rot.

"Fresh without fragrance

the tulip was."

Humbert Wolfe

Things My Mother Never Told Me

- If you live in a rainy part of the country, dig up ranunculus tubers. They do not like to be soaked.
- Many bulbs such as gladiolus corms and narcissus bulbs multiply in the ground. If possible, do not dig them up.
- Forced bulbs, with the exception of amaryllis, will not bloom a second year, but they may be planted outdoors in the garden where they might eventually bloom again.

A SHORT DISSERTATION ON BULBS

Forcing Bulbs to Bloom Out of Season

- A cheerful sight in the bleak winter months when a blizzard is howling and moaning outside, is a window filled with spring flowers. Bulbs can be forced to bloom out of season by controlling temperature and light. Bulbs which are usually forced are the tender bulbs such as daffodils, narcissus, hyacinths, crocus and amaryllis.
- Forced bulbs can be planted in anything from an old copper frying pan to Aunt Emma's chamber pot.
- Bulbs can be placed in a prepared planting mix or in water and pebbles. Hyacinths are often grown in water in special vases made for this purpose.
- After bulbs have been planted, place them in a dark, cool place. Hyacinth vases may be stored in the refrigerator.
- Bulbs should develop a good root system before moving them into the daylight.
- When the root system is well established and the top growth is about 2" high, put plant in full light in a cool room, but keep it out of the direct sun for a few days until it becomes acclimated. If a plant is left in the dark too long, its leaves become "leggy".
- In a few weeks plants will bloom and you can make mint juleps and pretend it's spring.

Individual bulbs are discussed in mini-chapters under their specific names.

11

MUCH ADO ABOUT FERNS

**F**erns are non-flowering plants and are to many a gardener what diamonds are to girls - they are their best friends because they have very few hang-ups and insects and pests seldom go near them. Their care is so minimal as to be practically non-existent. They are perennials which grow and thrive in dark corners of the garden where even weeds must struggle for survival. Many ferns in cold areas are deciduous. Plants condescendingly reproduce by spores, which are found on the underside of each frond, the name for a fern leaf.

Some of the most popular and decorative ones are Boston Fern, Australian and Tasmanian Tree Ferns, Maidenhair Fern, Bear's Foot Fern, Squirrel's Foot Fern, Rabbit's Paw Fern, and Deer Fern.

"A plant is like a self-willed man, out of whom we can obtain all which we desire, if we will only treat him his own way."

Goethe

Planting
- Best time for planting, or dividing clumps when they get crowded, is in early spring or fall.
- Plant in partial or full shade in a moist, rich soil that has been replenished with peat moss or leafmold.
- Do not bury the crowns. An exception to this rule are rhizomes, which grow horizontally along or just under the ground. Plant these 1"-2" deep.

Care
- Keep soil moist, but do not let it get soggy.
- Feed with a fish emulsion during growing season.
- When the temperature is hot, sprinkle ferns with water early in the morning or in the evening.
- If roots become exposed, in hot weather mulch them with peat moss. In cold areas, mulch plants with leaves in the winter.

12

GROUND COVERS

A **Short Treatise on Evolution**
Scientists say that zillions of years ago the earth was a round, flaming mass of matter whirling through space. Trillions of years ago the earth slowed down. Volcanoes began belching debris and land emerged from the oceans. There was much heaving and swaying. Later - a few billion years - the volcanoes became relatively quiet and lush ground covers began growing on the land. Living organisms crawled from the oceans, and millions of years later they developed into multitudes of different plants and animals. The animals ate the plants. Thousands of years later man evolved from the animals. Man ate the plants and also the animals.

As the above proves, ground covers have been around for some time. Today they are the Persian, Oriental, and Aubusson rugs of the garden. They tie together and make a total entity out of separate components such as trees, flower beds, and grass. They also soften the lines of a building or a terrace, and are useful in preventing soil erosion on banks and hillsides.

Hundreds of plants are used as ground covers. Some hug the soil and others grow 2' high. Many have berries and flowers. Most require little care except for an occasional trimming and feeding.

The following are just a few of the many genera, species, and varieties of ground covers. Plants that thrive in the sun, in sun and shade, or only in the shade are listed under separate headings. In some climates they might come under different headings. Consult your nurseryman. He will tell you which ones are best for your area and for your needs.

GROUND COVERS

Ground Covers for Sunny Areas

• **African Daisy, Freeway Daisy** (*Osteospermum fruticosum*)
Flowers are light purple the first day and off-white the second. They
open only when the sun shines. Plants stand lots of neglect and are very
sturdy and spread rapidly.

• **Gazania** (*Gazania rigens leucolaena*)
Foliage is silvery gray and flowers are orange, bronze, yellow, red, pink,
and white. They resemble daisies and close when the sun goes down.
Plants are very sturdy and spread rapidly.

• **Ice Plant**
There are many genera and species of ice plants, but some that are
particularly good for ground covers are *Delosperma*, *Lampranthus*, and
Malephora crocea.

• **Juniper** (*Juniperus*)
Some junipers are a few inches high and others grow 2'-3' high.
All have needle-like foliage. The Blue Carpet Juniper (*Juniperus
horizontalis* 'Wiltonii') is the flattest and has silver-blue foliage on long
trailing branches.

• **Lily Turf** (*Liriope spicata*)
Leaves are a dark green and resemble blades of grass. Small flowers are
pale lilac and white. Good in cold areas. Will grow in partial shade.

• **Oregano** (*Origanum vulgare*)
In mild climates this herb makes an excellent ground cover in non-
manicured places. It is fast growing and will take over an area if runners
are not controlled. The small flowers are purple. Cut plants back once a
year after the flowers have bloomed.

• **Phlox, Moss Pink** (*phlox subulata*)
Flowers are in various shades of pink, a light purple-blue, and white.
New hybrids are constantly being developed. Moderately resistant to
droughts. Cut plants back after blooming.

GROUND COVERS

- **Snow-in-Summer** (*Cerastium tomentosum*)

Silvery gray leaves and white flowers. Fast growing in all climates. Plant in partial shade in hot areas.

- **Thyme, Mother-of-Thyme** (*Thymus praecox arcticus*)

Good for small areas. The fragrant leaves are a dark green and the small flowers have a purple hue.

- **Vinca** (*Vinca major*)

Excellent for large areas. Leaves are dark green or white-variegated. Flowers are a lavender blue. Plants spread rapidly and should be kept under control. They can be cut back to the ground, and new growth will soon appear.

"Speak not - whisper not;

here bloweth thyme

and bergamot."

Samuel Coleridge

Ground Covers for Sunny and Shady Areas

- **Ajuga, Bugleweed, Carpet Bugle** (*Ajuga reptans*)

Foliage is green, purplish green, or bronze. Spikes of flowers are blue, white, and pink. Fast growing. Excellent under trees. Very colorful.

- **Cotoneaster, Bearberry** (*Cotoneaster dammeri*)

Plants have red fruit, and are hardy and fast growing. They like to cascade over walls.

- **Honeysuckle, Hall's Japanese Honeysuckle** (*Lonicera japonica*)

This is a sturdy plant that grows fast and will climb trees and fences if permitted. Good for large, steep areas. Fairly resistant to droughts. Flowers are white, changing to yellow.

- **Indian Mock Strawberry** (*Duchesnea indica*)

Best grown under trees and shrubs as plants grow rapidly and will take over any bed. Tiny yellow flowers turn into miniature strawberries, but they are not good for eating.

GROUND COVERS

- **Ivy** (*Hedera*)

This is one of the most popular of all ground covers. Many are variegated. Some of the species are English Ivy (*Hedera helix*), Algerian Ivy (*Hedera canariensis*), and Persian Ivy (*Hedera colchica*). 'Baltica', an English Ivy, is the hardiest of them all. Snails love to hide under the leaves of all species.

- **Ivy Geranium** (*Pelargonium peltatum*)

Thrives in mild climates where plants are often used in place of lawns. The single or double flowers are white, lilac, and many shades of pink. Plants become scraggly if they are not cut back from time to time.

- **Plumbago, Dwarf Plumbago** (*Ceratostigma plumbaginoides*)

Very hardy and easy to grow. Excels for color under and around shrubs or in full sun. Has tiny clusters of cobalt blue flowers that bloom in summer and fall. Shining green leaves turn bronze in fall.

- **Sedum, Stonecrop**

Members of this genus are succulent perennials. There are many different species in this group of plants. Two that are used as ground covers are Goldmoss (*Sedum acre*), and Dragon's Blood (*Sedum spurium*).

Ground Covers for Shady Areas

- **Baby's Tears** (*Soleirolia soleirolii*)

The leaves are tiny and very fragile. Plants are rapid growers and are quick to recover when damaged. Will grow in full sun near seashores. Plants freeze in cold weather, but they come back. Good under ferns.

- **Vinca, Dwarf Periwinkle** (*Vinca minor*)

Will grow in sun in some areas. Flowers are white and various shades of blue. Very hardy and fast growing.

- **Pachysandra, Japanese Spurge** (*Pachysandra terminalis*)

White flowers turn into small white fruit. Leaves are a deep green or are variegated.

13

SUCCULENTS

 ucculents are often associated with dusty, hot deserts and bewhiskered miners searching for Golconda. Many are not indigenous to deserts and would die if forced to live in the blazing sun. Succulents are decorative plants with very low maintenance and care.

Basically, succulents are plants that store water in their fleshy leaves, stems or roots. Some authorities include many desert plants in this category even though these do not store water.

There are many genera of succulents. A few are: Sedum, Kalanchoe, Crassula, Mesembryanthemum, Echeveria, Agave, Aloe, and Yucca. Cactus is usually classified under a separate category. Some succulents are large ornamental plants. Others have flashy flowers in brilliant colors. Many are used in rock gardens, as indoor plants, for controlling erosion on hillsides and banks, and for ground covers.

Planting
- Most prefer a sunny location, but many do not. Consult your nurseryman when in doubt.
- All succulents must have a loose, fast draining soil. Plants from arid regions prefer a soil with a light alkalinity.
- Plants look best when one variety is massed alone or when a pattern of different species is created. They do not combine well with other plants.

Care
- Water only when the soil is dry, and water infrequently during cold weather and when plants are dormant.
- If plants are in containers, feed once during the growth period with a well-balanced fertilizer.
- The fleshy succulents are easily propagated by cutting off stems and planting them in the ground or in pots.

14

HOW TO BEAT INFLATION BY PROPAGATION

Packets of seeds cost much less than small, established plants, but lots of patience and effort is required to achieve the same happy ending. The following are a few ways to beat inflation by propagating your own plants. These methods are for adventurous gardeners with time on their hands and hope in their hearts.

Growing Plants from Seeds

Three Mediums
- Many gardeners have their favorite mediums for propagating seeds. My gardening friend with the high rubber boots chooses any of the following:
    1. Sterile, coarse sand.
    2. Equal parts of sand, vermiculite and sphagnum moss.
    3. A prepared mixture of potting soil.
- All mediums should be 1"-2" deep and kept moist at all times but never soggy.

Containers
- Flats, egg cartons, aluminum or plastic pans with holes in the bottoms, shallow wooden boxes, pots, and seed trays all make good containers for sowing.

Sowing
- Seeds can be sown in small, shallow trenches and covered with a thin layer of medium, or they can be carefully scattered and covered to a depth twice their own diameter.
- Many large seeds are sown directly in the ground.

Prices are going up, up, up like a hot air balloon.

About the only things that are coming down are leaves in the fall, an occasional meteor, rain, and the sky on Chicken Little.

PROPAGATION

After Sowing

- Gently firm seeds by lightly pressing soil with a board or the bottom of a flower pot. If soil dries out and needs moisture, water from below by placing container in a pan of water, or from the top with a fine spray.
- Slow sprouting seeds are often covered with plastic or glass. These should be removed for a couple of minutes every few days unless they are ventilated. Completely remove coverings when small, green shoots appear.
- Keep in a warm, light, dry spot out of the direct sun. A very low heat applied to the bottom of the container helps seeds germinate.
- Transplant or thin out seedlings when the first true, or second set of leaves, develop. Keep out of direct sunlight for a few more days and keep soil moist but not damp. Damping Off, a fungus disease, often attacks seedlings if soil is too moist or circulation is not good.
- In a few weeks or a month, seedlings will be ready to be transplanted to their permanent place, if they are not already there.

Growing Plants from Softwood and Semi-Hardwood Cuttings

- Softwood cuttings are the easiest and fastest to grow and are made from new growth that snaps off easily when it is bent. Semi-hardwood cuttings are from new growth that has matured a few months but still snaps off easily. There are also hardwood cuttings which are taken from trees and shrubs.
- Spring and early summer are the best times to start cuttings.
- Make cuttings from strong, healthy stems with good growth at their tips. Make a slanted cut with a sharp, sterile instrument just below a node. Cuttings should have 3 to 5 nodes on them and should be from 4"-6" long. Remove all large leaves, buds, and leaves from bottom nodes.

"Flower in the crannied wall, I pluck you out of the crannies, I hold you here, root and all, in my hand, Little flower - but if I could understand What you are, root and all, and all in all, I should know what God and man is."

Alfred, Lord Tennyson

PROPAGATION

- Dip cuttings in a rooting hormone powder and place one half of the stems in the soil. Use the same rooting mediums as for growing seeds. Many cuttings can also be rooted in water or directly in the ground.
- Place a plastic covering or an inverted glass jar over them. Remove these for a few minutes every two or three days unless there is ventilation. Many cuttings do not need the extra humidity these coverings provide.
- Place in a warm, light place out of the direct sun and keep cuttings moist but not wet.
- From 4 to 8 weeks cuttings usually develop good root systems and new shoots begin to grow. They are now ready to be transplanted to their permanent place.

Growing Plants from Root Cuttings

- Roots that produce sprouts will produce new plants from root cuttings.
- Cut a healthy root into 2"-3" sections. Place these sections horizontally in a rooting medium and cover with a thin layer of soil. Thoroughly water and cover with newspaper, glass, or plastic. Keep in a shady place and keep soil moist.
- Remove covering when new sprouts appear. When new growth is a few inches high, roots can be planted in the ground or in pots.
- Cuttings can also be placed upright in pots. Place the thickest end of the roots just at soil level and treat the same as the ones grown horizontally.

Other Methods of Growing Plants

- Plants can also be propagated by leaf cuttings, air layering, ground layering, budding, and grafting. All but the first method take lots of skill and practice and are for the advanced gardener.

"The first day of spring was once time for taking the young virgins into the fields, there in dalliance to set an example in fertility for Nature to follow. Now we just set the clock an hour ahead and change the oil in the crankcase."

E. B. White

AGAPANTHUS, LILY-OF-THE-NILE
Agapanthus orientalis

Agapanthus plants remind me of Cleopatra floating down the
Nile on her royal barge. Nubian slaves are slowly moving large
fans of peacock feathers to create a cool breeze. Is that Anthony
or is it Caesar on the couch beside her?

These plants are very sturdy and require little care. They add an aristocratic touch to a garden with their tall stems and large clusters of flowers
swaying in a gentle wind. Their roots are tuberous and they readily
multiply. Plants grow in large clumps of long, thin evergreen leaves.
Flowers bloom in summer and are various shades of beautiful blues and
white. The most popular species is Agapanthus orientalis with 5' stems.
'Peter Pan' is another favorite with 1' stems.

Planting
- In mild climates, plant in early spring or fall. In cold climates,
  plant in tubs or pots in spring.
- Do not divide plants for at least six years as they like to be
  crowded and hate to be moved. Divide them after they have
  bloomed. They often do not bloom the following year after
  being divided.
- Plants need some sun during the day to bloom, but do not plant
  in full sun in hot areas.
- They prefer a loamy soil with good drainage, but will survive in
  heavy soils.

Care
- Water deeply once a week from spring to early fall and feed once
  a month with a balanced fertilizer.
- Cut off flowers after blooming before seed pods form.

AGERATUM, FLOSS FLOWER
Ageratum houstonianum

Ageratums are small, dainty annuals with tiny clusters of lavender, white, or pink flowers that bloom all summer. In mild climates they bloom longer. Plants are good as borders or mixed with other flowers in pots or containers. They grow 4"-12" high depending upon the variety. Dwarf varieties are 4"-6" high.

Planting
- Plant in full sun. In hot climates plant in partial shade.
- Plant in a rich soil in spring. In mild climates can also be planted in late summer for fall color, or in the fall for spring color.

Care
- Almost pest free except for snails. Needs little care.
- Water often and feed once a month with a fish emulsion or a balanced fertilizer.
- After blooming, cut back and plants might bloom again.
- Plants often reseed themselves.

How to Make a Colorful Fourth of July Basket
- Line a basket with heavy, clear plastic and put in some prepared planting soil.
- Fill with white petunias, lavender ageratums, and red verbenas.
- Tie balloons filled with helium to the handle and put several small American flags among the plants.
- Many other combinations of red, white, and blue flowers can be used.
- Do not keep plants in basket for more than a week as there is no drainage and the roots will rot.

ALYSSUM, SWEET ALYSSUM
Lobularia maritima

You bet your sweet alyssum this dainty looking annual makes an excellent ground cover or border. It is also a staple in window boxes and planters. Plants require little care and readily reseed themselves. They grow wild in many parts of the country - and in many gardens! Tiny clusters of white, lavender, or pinkish-lavender flowers bloom almost all year in mild climates. In others, they bloom in spring and summer. There are many different varieties from 2"-12" high. A popular one is 'Carpet of Snow' which grows 2"-4" high.

Planting
- In mild climates, can be planted almost any time. In other climates, plant in early spring.
- Plant in full sun. Will tolerate partial shade.
- Not particular about type of soil. Plant young plants from nurseries about 4" apart.
- In mild climates, plants reseed themselves in cracks in the pavement and crannies in the wall.

Care
- Needs practically no care.
- Cut back plants after they have bloomed. This keeps them from getting straggly, and another crop of flowers will quickly grow.

AMARYLLIS, NAKED LADY, BELLADONNA LILY*

Amaryllis belladonna

Childish Behavior

When my son was small and belladonna lilies were in bloom, he would come running into the house shouting, "There's a naked lady in the garden!" He grew up and stopped acting childish. I am ashamed to say my husband, who is a successful, well-respected businessman, still comes running into the house every August and announces, "There's a naked lady in the garden!"

The common name for amaryllis is Naked Lady. They amuse me because first you see them - then you don't - and then you do. They are bulbs that have clumps of green leaves in the fall and winter. In the late spring the leaves completely die away and nothing is left above the ground. Soon spikes begin to appear. In August when they are 2'-3' high, clusters of rosy-pink flowers shaped like trumpets burst into bloom. After they fade, plants are dormant for a short time before new foliage begins to grow and the cycle starts again. Flowers will not bloom in climates that do not have warm, dry summers.

"In naked beauty

more adorn'd more

lovely than Pandora."

John Milton

Planting

- Plant bulbs in the fall.
- In mild climates, plants are so hardy they will grow in sun or partial shade and in almost any type of soil. In cold climates, plant in tubs or pots and bring inside for the winter.

Care

- Plants are drought resistant and thrive on neglect.
- Most bugs ignore them, but snails like to hide in their leaves.
- Plants need to be divided when they get crowded, but do this only when it is necessary as they do not like to be disturbed. If they are moved at the wrong time, they will not bloom for several years. The best time to divide them is in the fall after they have bloomed. Never divide them when they are dormant, which is in the late spring and early summer.

* Amaryllis is also the common name for another bulb whose genus is *Hippeastrum*.

ANEMONE, POPPY-FLOWERED ANEMONE   *Anemone coronaria*

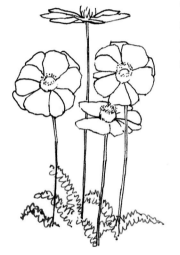

Anemones have tuberous roots and are perennials. In many areas they do not bloom well the second year and are treated as annuals. There are several species of anemones, but this is the flashiest and the most popular one. The flowers resemble poppies. They are single, double or semidouble, and bloom from early spring to fall, depending upon the area. Plants do not do well in very hot or very cold climates.

Planting

- In mild climates plant tubers in October or November. In cold climates, plant in spring.
- Plant in a spot where flowers do not get full sun all day.
- Do not soak tubers before planting. This can be disastrous in areas where it rains a lot. Anemones will do much better if they are well watered when planted, and not watered again until foliage appears. Plants are very susceptible to root rot. Many gardeners start anemones in flats of moist sand so they can control the moisture. Plants are transferred to the garden when they are about 3" high.
- Plant tubers with rounded side up and pointed side down. Plant l"-2" deep and about a foot apart in a rich soil with good drainage.

These are very patriotic

plants as the flowers are

either red, white, or blue.

Care

- Birds, snails, slugs, and rabbits love the foliage. Place a wire covering over tubers after planting, and put snail bait out before the leaves appear.
- Feed with a balanced fertilizer when foliage begins to grow.
- After plants have bloomed and foliage has withered, dig up the tubers and dry them for a few days in the sun. Clean them and store in a well-ventilated spot. In mild climates they can be left in the ground.

ASTER, CHINA ASTER
Callistephus chinensis

There are over 600 species of perennial asters, but the common aster in summer gardens is an annual. The plants look delicate and frail, but they are sturdy, if they are a wilt resistant strain.

There are many different varieties of the common aster. Plants grow 1'-3' high. Some of the flowers resemble peonies and anemones, and others are shaped like pompons. My favorite ones look like feathers from a rare bird. Flowers are white and many different shades of pink and lavender.

Planting
- Plant a foot apart in the spring or early summer in full sun. Will grow in most soils, but drainage must be good as plants are subject to stem rot. A sandy soil is preferable.

Care
- Pinch back young plants when they are about 6" high to make them bushy and produce more flowers.
- Do not overwater plants, and feed them with a well-balanced fertilizer every two weeks before buds form. Then switch to a high-bloom fertilizer (2-10-10).
- Stake if necessary.
- Plants are subject to a virus called aster yellows. Destroy infected plants. Mildew and wilt also often attack them, particularly in the fall. Spray or dust with sulphur.
- Do not plant asters in the same spot two years in a row.

Asters remind me of my favorite maiden aunt. She is very fragile looking and old-fashioned, but she is quite a dame.

AZALEA, Rhododendron

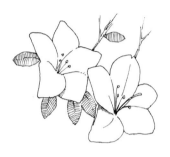

Azaleas are deciduous or evergreen shrubs which grow from 1'-20' high depending upon the species. The most popular ones for the garden are the evergreen hybrids. Deciduous azaleas have spectacular blooms, and their leaves actually turn autumn colors at the proper time. Hundreds of varieties of azaleas have been propagated to thrive in many different climates from cold to hot. Your local nurseryman will tell you which ones are best for your area.

Planting

If you want to be dazzled

by acres of azalea shrubs in

full bloom, go to the Deep

South or the Pacific

Northwest in the spring.

- Plant in the fall or early winter when shrubs are dormant.
- Azaleas like an acid soil with good drainage. Add leaf mold, peat moss, or ground bark to a heavy, clay soil.
- Plant with top of root ball just above level of soil. The shallow, fibrous roots need more oxygen than most plants.
- Plant in filtered shade. In areas where summers are not too hot, they can be planted in full sun. New sun resistant strains have been developed.
- Give plants plenty of room to grow in. Remember, they are shrubs.

Care

- Feed with an acid fertilizer when new growth begins in the spring and again after plants have bloomed. Then feed monthly until August. There are many fertilizers formulated just for azaleas.
- Keep plants well watered in the early summer when new growth is forming. During the rest of the year, keep soil moist but never let it get soggy.
- Never weed with a hoe near the plants as the roots grow close to the surface and they might get injured.
- Pinch back the tips of new growth that appears after the blooming period if you do not want plants to get larger or if you want to shape them.

BABY'S BREATH
Gypsophila paniculata

I like the name of this plant because it is so graphic. Cloud Nine would also be an appropriate name as the wispy puffs of flower clusters seem to float in the air. I also like its botanical name, *Gypsophila paniculata*. It has a lot of panache and rolls off the tongue with a lyrical sound. Baby's breath has been indispensible to florists for decades as a filler of empty spaces in arrangements. In the garden it is used as a contrast for large leafed plants and flamboyant ones such as oriental poppies and delphiniums.

Some species of gypsophila are annuals, but this one is a perennial that grows 3'-4' high. The clusters of hundreds of tiny, single or double flowers are white, pink and rose. They bloom from June to October.

Planting
- Plant young plants 2' apart in the spring in full sun.
- Not particular about soil so long as it isn't acid.

Care
- Feed young plants with a well-balanced fertilizer.
- Stake large clumps if necessary.
- If flowers are cut back after blooming and before seeds form, plants should bloom again.
- Cut plants back completely when blooming season is through.
- Can be propagated from stem cuttings and division of clumps.
- Flowers can be dried for winter bouquets. For best results cut flowers before they are fully opened and hang them upside down in a well-ventilated, dark place.

BACHELOR'S BUTTON, CORNFLOWER, BLUEBOTTLE, RAGGED SAILOR

Centaurea cyanus

The numerous revealing and endearing pseudonyms of this flower are proof it is a great favorite. It is an annual that grows 1' - 2' high and is often grown in cutting gardens because plants are not too attractive. They have grayish leaves and flowers are single or double. The most popular color is blue, but there are varieties that are various shades of pink and purple. There is also a white. They bloom profusely from July until the frosts. Plants often become scraggly and mangy looking at the end of the season.

Planting

- Young plants are available at nurseries in spring. In mild climates, also in fall. Seeds are large and can be sown directly in the ground. They germinate in ten days and will bloom in two months from the time of sowing.
- Plant in full sun 8" - 10" apart in a light soil with good drainage.

Care

- Plants do best when neglected. Do not feed very often.
- Keep flowers picked for more bloom.
- Plants are hardy but are subject to rust, root rot, and the "yellows". Dust with sulphur for rust, and destroy plants with root rot and the "yellows".

"Marriage has many pains, but celibacy has no pleasures."

Samuel Johnson

BEGONIA, BEDDING OR WAX
Begonia semperflorens-cultorum

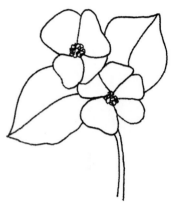

I will always have begonias in my garden. They are accommodating, attractive plants that are used as borders, bedding plants, or in containers. Once planted they need little or no care.

There are hundreds of species and varieties of begonias, but the one discussed here is the popular bedding or wax begonia. Plants are perennials, but in cold climates, they are grown as annuals or in pots. They thrive near the sea where summers are cool, but they can be grown very successfully in other areas.

Plants are low growing and have fibrous roots and glossy, succulent leaves and stems. There are tall (15"), medium (10") and dwarf (5") varieties. The single or double flowers are different shades of pink, red, white, yellow and bi-colored. They bloom profusely in the summer and fall, and in mild climates they bloom off and on all year. The leaves are various shades of green, bronze, dark red, or variegated.

Planting
- In mild climates, they can be planted almost all year round. In cold climates, plant in spring.
- Can be planted in full sun near the sea, but prefers filtered shade elsewhere. Plants with darker leaves and flowers can take more sun.
- Plant 6"-8" apart in a rich soil with good drainage and one slightly on the acid side.

Care
- Keep plants well watered.
- Feed regularly with a well-balanced fertilizer.
- Divide plants when they get crowded.
- Begonias can easily be propagated by stem cuttings which are rooted in water, sand, or directly in the soil.

BELLS-OF-IRELAND
Moluccella laevis

Bells-of-Ireland are aptly named because they are full of malarky. They aren't really bell-shaped and are not from Ireland. They are annuals with 2' spikes that are covered with apple-green "bells" or "shells". Plants are a good contrast for brilliantly colored flowers in the garden, and the fascinating spikes are long-lasting in arrangements. They bloom in the summer.

Planting
- Plants do not transplant well, so it is best to start them from seed.
- Refrigerate seeds about a week before planting. In the early spring sow seeds directly in the ground where they are to grow. In mild climates, this can also be done in the fall. Seeds will take about a month to germinate.
- Not particular about type of soil, but there should be good drainage. Plant in a sunny location.

Care
- Feed regularly with a well-balanced fertilizer.
- Keep plants well watered.
- Spikes can be dried for winter bouquets. First remove the leaves and then hang spikes upside down in a cool, dark spot with good ventilation.

Bells-of-Ireland

are as Irish as

Ella Fitzgerald!

BIRD-OF-PARADISE
Strelitzia reginae

Clandestine Shenanigans

Birds-of-paradise are extremely prolific in Southern California. Plants are found along highways, byways, driveways, in gardens and parks, and around department stores and supermarkets. An organization called "The Midnight Supply Company" should be formed in this area to fulfill the needs of the flower marts in New York City where one stem of these flowers sells at an astronomically high price. If the pickers were not apprehended by the law, the company could net a fortune.

Plants thrive in temperate climates, and are perennials. They grow 4'-5' high in large clumps, and the flowers bloom from October until late spring. In cold climates, plants must be grown in containers and brought inside for the winter.

This glamorous plant has a perfect name as the flowers resemble heads of exotic orange, blue and white tropical birds.

Planting
- Plants can be bought in gallon cans at nurseries, or established plants can be divided to start new ones.
- Plant in full sun. Not particular about type of soil.
- Plant 5' apart in groups or in rows along a fence or driveway. They also make a good background in flower beds.

Care
- Feed occasionally with a well-balanced fertilizer or a fish emulsion.
- In hot weather, deep water at least once a week.
- Protect plants when low temperatures are expected.
- Snails love to hide at the bottom of the leaves and they nibble on the flowers. Put out snail bait before flowers bloom.
- Plants do not like to be disturbed and do best when crowded. Divide after the blooming period and only when necessary.

BLANKET FLOWER, GAILLARDIA
Gaillardia grandiflora

Gaillardias are as American as the "Stars and Stripes" and a Fourth of July Parade, but they are named after a Frenchman, Gaillard de Marentonneau, an 18th-century botanist. One species is native to the Central and Western part of the country.

Plants are perennials and love the sun and heat. They are very easy to grow. There are many varieties of this species of gaillardia, which is a hybrid. Some are dwarf size and some grow 4' high. The flowers are on long stems and are single or double with maroon or orange bands. There are many different shades of yellow and red. They bloom from June to November and are great for cutting or as a splash of color in the garden. Plants reseed themselves.

Nebraska is aflame in

the summertime with

gaillardias in full bloom.

Planting
- Young plants are available at nurseries in the spring or fall. Seeds are also easy to sow right in the ground.
- Plant in full sun about 1' apart. This will vary with size of plant. Place tall ones at the back of beds and surround them with other plants as their foliage is sparse.
- Not particular about type of soil, but should have good drainage. Plants will not survive if soil is soggy.

Care
- Occasionally feed with a well-balanced fertilizer.
- Do not overwater and keep faded flowers picked.
- Some of the taller plants might need to be staked.
- Root cuttings can be made in early spring.

BLEEDING HEART, DICENTRA
Dicentra spectabilis

Bleeding Heart sounds more like the title of a book written by Dr. Christiaan Barnard or Dr. Dudley White than the name of a perennial plant that has dainty, heart-shaped flowers and lacy, fern-like leaves. The small, rosy pink flowers are on 2'-3' stems, and they bloom in the late spring. Plants disappear in the winter and reappear again the following spring. Most varieties like cold climates and shady places, but many will grow in mild climates.

Planting
- Dormant roots are available at local nurseries in the late fall to early spring.
- Plant in a cool, shady location in a rich soil with good drainage.
- Can be planted in groups or naturalized under trees and shrubs. They mix well with ferns and other shade loving plants.

Care
- Keep plants moist, but do not let the soil get soggy.
- Feed regularly with a well-balanced fertilizer.
- In the winter when plants die back, mark their location so they will not be harmed by a tool, or dug up.
- Roots can be divided for new plants. Do this after the blooming period.
- In mild climates, plants are often treated as annuals.

CACTUS

- Cactus grows wild in the Southwestern part of the United States, and from horizon to horizon, there are miles and miles of many varieties of this plant.

- Cactus has many sharp spines that hurt upon contact.

- I sat on a cactus plant twenty years ago.

- I hate cactus.

- If you want to find out about cactus, go to the nearest library or arboretum.

CALENDULA, POT MARIGOLD
Calendula officinalis

Calendulas are easy to grow and are sturdy, prolific annuals that need little care. They worship the sun and bring cheer to a garden. Flowers are bright yellow, soft yellow, strong orange, apricot, and cream. One variety has dark centers and resembles black-eyed susan daisies. Plants are 1'-2' high. In mild areas, flowers bloom from late fall to early summer. In cold climates, from spring to late summer.

Planting
- In cold climates, plant in the early spring for spring and mid-summer bloom. In mild climates, plant in the fall.
- Not particular about type of soil, but must be in a sunny location.
- Plant in groups, in borders, or mix with other sun loving flowers.

Care
- Pinch back young plants when they are 6" high. This will make plants branch out and produce more flowers.
- Keep flowers picked for more bloom. Pick flowers for arrangements when the petals are half open as blooms do not last long.
- Watch for mildew, which is the curse of calendulas. Avoid overhead watering.
- When plants become leggy and flowers become small, toss everything into the trash or compost heap.

If you can't grow calendulas, give up gardening and take up crocheting or croquet!

CALLA, COMMON CALLA, CALLA LILY
Zantedeschia aethiopica

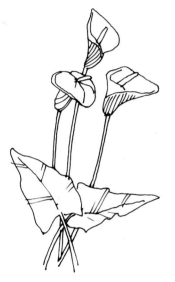

For decades callas were associated with death and funerals. Today they are a symbol of simplicity, and vases of these flowers are often found on coffee tables in sophisticated, modern settings.

Callas are rhizomes, which grow horizontally on or just under the soil. They will not survive cold winters, but are quite easy to grow in mild climates where they multiply and reproduce at an indecent rate.

There are many species of callas. This one is the Common Calla and is popular with gardeners and florists. Flowers are white and creamy white, and bloom on stems 1'-2' long. In mild climates they bloom in late winter and spring until hot weather arrives. In cold climates they bloom in late spring and midsummer.

Other species of callas are the Golden Calla, the Pink or Red Calla, and the Spotted Calla. Many new hybrids are being developed.

Planting
- In cold climates plant in early spring. In mild climates plant in fall or early spring.
- Place rhizomes horizontally with the eyes up and plant 4"-6" deep and 1' apart in partial shade.
- Plants prefer a soil that retains moisture.

Care
- Callas require very little care, but they do like lots of water. After blooming, water sparingly until new growth begins.
- During their growing season, feed once a month with a balanced fertilizer.
- After blooming, leaves often droop and yellow. Trim them back when new growth begins to appear.
- In cold climates, dig up plants after blooming period and store rhizomes until the following spring.

CAMELLIA
Camellia japonica, C. sasanqua, C. reticulata

Camellias are slow growing, acid loving shrubs. Some experts claim there are less than a dozen species while others say there are at least thirty! However, everyone agrees that there are over 4,000 named varieties of this exquisite flower. They are easy to grow if you live in one of the Pacific Coast states, in the South, or in some parts of Texas.

More than 200 years ago, Europeans discovered camellias growing wild in Japan, China, and on islands along the coast of Asia. Long before the Civil War, more than 100 varieties were growing in the Magnolia Gardens near Charleston, and some of these plants are still alive and well!

Almost all camellias grown by amateur gardeners belong to three species. Following are the names and a brief description of each.

"A thing of beauty

is a joy forever"

John Keats

Camellia japonica
This is by far the most popular species. Plants grow 6'-12' high, but they can reach 20'. There are several hundred varieties of japonicas, and the colors of the flowers are different shades of red, pink, white, and many are variegated. The blooms are single, semi-double, double, peony form, anemone form, rose form, "rabbit ears" (fluted petals), and fimbriata (fringed edges on the petals). The blooming period for these flowers varies according to the variety and the location. Generally speaking: in Washington and Oregon, japonicas bloom in March and April; in California they bloom in February and March, and in the South in January and February - and also March in North and South Carolina.

A new variety called 'Guilio Nuccio' is considered by many to be the best camellia ever to be developed. It has large, semidouble, coral-rose flowers. The inner petals are fluted. Some are variegated with fringed petals.

CAMELLIA

Camellia sasanqua

These plants are hardier than the japonicas and can be grown in colder climates. They bloom profusely in the fall and early winter. Plants are fast growers and are often used for hedges or for espaliers. Most varieties can stand full sun.

Camellia reticulata

This species has been popular in England since the early 1800s. Plants are lanky and not bushy, but the flowers are large and showy. They are best grown under very large trees such as oaks, pines, or magnolias. Most varieties have large, semidouble blooms with ruffled and fluted inner petals.

Planting

- Can be planted any time of the year except in very hot or very cold months.
- In areas with mild, cool summers, most varieties can be planted in full sun. In warmer sections, plant in partial shade.
- Always give plants lots of room. They live a long time and can eventually grow into large shrubs and trees if they are not pruned.
- Never plant camellias close to a concrete or white wall that reflects the afternoon sun.
- Plant in a fertile, acid soil that has good drainage. A good soil mixture is 1/2 soil, 1/4 peat moss, and 1/4 sand. Some gardeners prefer to use a mixture with mostly peat moss.
- Camellias are surface feeders and must not be planted with the crowns of the root ball below the level of the soil. Many growers recommend the crown be 2" above the ground.

CAMELLIA

Care

- Never allow soil to completely dry out. Keep soil moist, but not soggy. It is best to thoroughly soak plants once a week.
- Some growers recommend feeding right after the blooming period with an acid type food, and then again in three months. However, there are many fertilizers formulated just for camellias and instructions on the packages should be followed.
- For larger flowers disbud all terminal buds to one or two. If possible, leave buds of various sizes to stagger the bloom.
- Plants often drop their buds if they are overwatered or under-watered. A sudden change of temperature can also cause this. Remove all buds and blooms that have fallen beneath plants to help prevent disease.
- Prune just after the blooming period, or when picking the flowers.
- Fewer pests bother camellias than most plants. However, camel-lia petal blight is a disease that often strikes. Flowers turn a mushy brown. Remove infected flowers and clean all debris from under plants. Spray with benomyl.

CANDYTUFT

Iberis sempervirens

Chauncey The Squirrel

Once upon a time, there was a young squirrel named Chauncey. He lived with his mother and father and three sisters in a very comfortable house at the top of a tall eucalyptus tree. One day Chauncey asked his mother if he could pick some ripe olives on a nearby tree. Mr. Arrid, his friend the skunk, had told him about it. His mother gave him permission, but she told him to be home before nightfall.

Chauncey leapt from tree to tree and finally reached the one filled with juicy, ripe olives. He clamped a delicious olive between his two front feet and began to eat. He chewed and munched until his tummy was full. He then decided to take a short nap before starting home to dinner. "Dinner! Ugh! I won't be able to eat again for weeks," he said to a butterfly who happened to flutter by just at that moment.

Soon he was fast asleep. Much later he was awakened by a loud woof. A small, black dog with very curly hair was prancing around the base of the tree. Chauncey looked at the sky. The sun was just about to set and it would soon be dark.

He quickly got up and leapt from tree to tree with the speed of the wind during a hurricane. He had promised his mother he would be back before nightfall, but the sun went down and all was black. Chauncey couldn't find the tall eucalyptus tree where he lived in a very comfortable house with his mother and father and three sisters. Then he remembered something his mother had told him a long time ago. "My dear son," she had said, "There are many, many eucalyptus trees where we live and they all look alike. I have planted a small patch of candytuft around the base of our tree. You will be able to see this patch even on the darkest of nights." Chauncey climbed to the very tip top of the tree he was in and looked around for a patch of snowy white flowers. There it was under the very next tree. He was home in seconds.

Moral of story - If you want to be sure you will always find your home, even on the darkest of nights, plant a patch of snowy white candytuft around your front door.

CANDYTUFT

Candytufts are perennials with snowy white clusters of flowers that bloom in the spring. The small varieties such as 'Little Cushion' and 'Little Gem' are 4"- 6" high and make good borders or ground covers. They are also good container plants when mixed with other flowers. 'Snowflake' is a taller variety that grows about 10" high. These plants bloom in the spring and stop blooming when it gets hot.

Planting

- In cold climates, plant in the spring after the frosts. In mild climates, can be planted in the early spring or in the fall. Not particular about type of soil.
- Place 6"-9" apart in full or partial sun. Plants multiply and spread rapidly.

Care

- Plants like lots of water. Deep water regularly, and feed once a month with a well-balanced fertilizer.
- After blooming period, give plants a "haircut". Many times, they will bloom again.
- Divide plants when they get crowded.
- Can be propagated from cuttings.

CANNA

When "every leaf is on its tree", the cannas are in full bloom. They are tropical and subtropical plants with tuberous roots that thrive in areas where the summers are warm and hot. They are large and bold and could never be tucked quietly away in a corner of the garden. Because of their demanding presence, they are often planted in parks and massed in formal beds in large gardens. Cannas are effective in smaller gardens when used as a background or as borders along driveways. There are some smaller varieties that aren't so overpowering.

The leaves are shaped somewhat like banana leaves, and the brilliant flowers could be a rare bird to someone with a great imagination. The flowers do not last long in arrangements, but the leaves are used to create tropical effects.

For years, the flowers were only red, yellow or orange. Now many softer tones have been developed such as rose, salmon, cream, and white. Some are bi-colored. The leaves are either deep green or bronze. Tall varieties are about 5' high and the smaller ones are 2'-3' high.

"Summer days for me

When every leaf

is on its tree."

Christina Rossetti

Planting
- Plant 5" deep in a rich soil with good drainage in early spring after the frosts.
- Plant tall varieties 18"-24" apart and the small ones 10" apart in full sun.

Care
- Water heavily when blooming, and keep faded flowers picked.
- In the fall when the blooming season is over, cut plants back to about 6". They increase rapidly and can be divided at this time. In cold climates, dig up and store the tuberous roots for the winter.
- Plants are subject to bacterial rot. This disease begins while the leaves are still rolled and often attacks if the soil is heavy and there is little or no drainage.

CANTERBURY BELL, CUP-AND-SAUCER
Campanula medium

King Henry II vs. The Archbishop of Canterbury

King Henry II and Thomas à Becket, the Archbishop of Canterbury, had many quarrels over the power and authority of the church and the state. The king became so angry with the Archbishop he had him murdered. The Catholic church made Becket a saint, and pilgrims flocked to the cathedral at Canterbury to pay him homage. They bought little bells as souvenirs to take home. The flowers on a plant resembled these little bells and were given the name Canterbury Bell.

Canterbury Bells are annuals or biennials. The single and double flowers are shaped like bells or urns, and are on 2'-4' high stems. Colors are lavender, blue, pink, violet, and white. They bloom in May, June, and July in mild climates.

Planting
- In cold climates, plant in the early spring. In mild climates, plant in the early fall.
- Plant 15"-20" apart in partial shade in a rich soil that holds moisture.
- Because of their height, put plants in the back of a bed or along a fence or wall.
- Plants grown from seeds will not bloom profusely until the second year.

Care
- Feed regularly with a well-balanced fertilizer.
- Stake plants if needed.
- If rust attacks, spray or dust with zineb.

CARNATION, CLOVE PINK
Dianthus caryophyllus

The carnation is a symbol of authority and graciousness. Ushers at weddings and funerals wear them in their lapels, and florists love them. Unfortunately, the tall varieties are not very decorative in the garden, but they are sensational as cut flowers or in leis.

Carnations are perennials with a wondrous, spicy fragrance. The double flowers are pure white, soft pink, deep red, bright vermillion, soft yellow salmon, and variegated. They bloom in summer. There are two types of carnations, the florist and the border. The florist carnation is a tall plant 2'-3' high. The border carnation grows about 1' high and is a compact plant with many blooms.

Planting
- In mild climates, plant young plants in fall or spring. In cold climates, in spring.
- Plant in full sun, and in hot climates, in partial shade.
- Plant in a rich soil with good drainage, and put florist carnations 1 1/2 ' apart. Border ones should be 10" apart.

Care
- Carnations have weak stems and should be staked before the weight of the flowers breaks them. A round wire staking is the best.
- Do not overwater plants, and let soil dry out between waterings.
- Feed regularly with a balanced fertilizer.
- For large flowers, remove sidebuds and leave only center ones.
- After blooming period, cut back plants to a leaf bud so they are about 6"-10" high. Border carnations should be cut back to 3"-4" high.
- Carnations can be propagated by stem cuttings or by layering. See Chapter Fourteen.

CHRYSANTHEMUM
Chrysanthemum morifolium

Too Many Chrysanthemums

Before I had a cutting garden with a steady supply of flowers, I had blooming chrysanthemum plants throughout my house all year round as they are always available at nurseries, flower shops, and supermarkets. After blooming, I planted them in my garden. In a few years, I had chrysanthemums up to my chin. My husband finally said, "Please, dear, no more chrysanthemums!" Actually, he left out the please and the dear and added a few bleeps. My Old Gardening Friend with the High Rubber Boots was more direct. He told me to get rid of all of them and upgrade their quality. He gave me the catalogue of a famous grower, and I now have bewitching, beguiling, and bewildering varieties with enthrallingly massive flowers.

Plants are sturdy perennials, and there are many varieties with myriads of different shapes and sizes. Some bloom early in the fall, and some bloom late in the fall. Commercial growers force them to bloom the year round. Flowers are yellow, white, red, pink, bronze, purple, orange, and multicolored. They are classified according to the form of their flowers, and the following are a few of the classifications: Anemone, Button Pompon, Cascade, Cushion, Decorative, Exhibition, Feathery, Japanese, Pompon, Quill, Single or Daisy, Spider, and Spoon.

CHRYSANTHEMUM

Planting

- Young plants are available at nurseries in the spring. Old plants can also be divided and cuttings can be started at this time. See next page.
- Plant 18" apart in full sun in a loamy soil with good drainage. Place small varieties closer together. Put a pinch of bonemeal at the bottom of each hole to help produce a healthy plant.

Care

Chrysanthemums have been cultivated in China since 500 BC and in Japan since 800 AD.

- Pinch back plants by removing the top pair of leaves on each shoot. In warm climates, do this until the middle of August, and in cold climates until the middle of July. If a plant has been neglected, more than the top pair of leaves should be pinched back. This is referred to as the "hard pinch".
- Feed with a well-balanced fertilizer or a fish emulsion every two weeks.
- Plants have shallow roots and should be staked.
- For large blooms, leave one bud per stem and pinch off the others.
- When flowers fade and new growth appears around the base of the plants, cut stems back to ground. In cold climates plants can be dug up and stored in a warm spot. Leave a clump of soil around them and put peat moss over them to keep them moist. Do not let them dry out. Plant in spring after the frosts.

CHRYSANTHEMUM

For Latter-Day Luther Burbanks, or
How to Make Chrysanthemum Cuttings

In April or May, make 3"-4" cuttings from the tips of strong, new growth on established plants. Pinch off the top two leaves and remove the foliage below the bottom inch.

Dip the ends of cuttings in a rooting hormone or a fungicide and plant in a rooting medium as soon as possible. The National Chrysanthemum Society recommends a medium of 1/3 sphagnum peat moss and 2/3 perlite. Sand alone, sand and perlite, and other mediums can also be used.

At football games in the

Keep cuttings in a shady spot and keep them moist but not wet.
They will rot if overwatered. This is called damping off. Mist plants on warm days.

Roaring Twenties,

coeds wore enormous

If it is warm, cuttings will root in 10-14 days and can then be planted in the ground or in pots.

chrysanthemum flowers

Footnote: Please don't call chrysanthemums "mums". They are much too aristocratic for this appellation.

pinned to their

raccoon coats.

CHINESE LANTERN, WINTER CHERRY
Physalis alkekengi

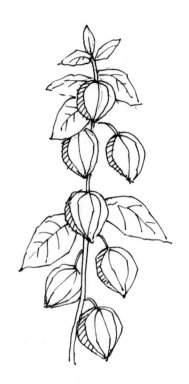

If only Chinese lanterns could be lighted! At night gardens would be turned into dazzling fairylands with thousands of twinkling lights. Every night the elves, gnomes, fairies, and leprechauns who live in every well-kept garden could dance and read until dawn.

Chinese Lanterns are rhizomes, which are thickened stems that grow horizontally along or under the surface of the soil. They are hardy perennials, but in cold areas, they are treated as annuals. The stems are filled with paper-like, vermilion pods which are shaped like lanterns. These are filled with scarlet berries. Plants grow about 2' high. A popular dwarf variety called 'Pygmy' grows 8" high and is an excellent plant for containers.

Planting
- Plant rhizomes about a foot apart in the spring in full sun or partial shade. In mild climates can be planted in the fall and winter.
- Not particular about type of soil, but prefers a light, sandy one.
- The rhizomes spread rapidly and will take over a bed. Plants also self-sow.

Care
- Needs little or no care.
- Stake plants before they start to droop.
- Can be divided in the fall or winter in mild climates, and in the spring in cold areas.

Things My Mother Never Told Me
- The dried pods are often used in winter flower arrangements. Dry them in the fall by placing stems in a horizontal position so the lanterns will hang to the side. The leaves can be removed for an oriental effect. Keep in a warm, dry, dark place until dried.

CHRISTMAS ROSE
Helleborus niger

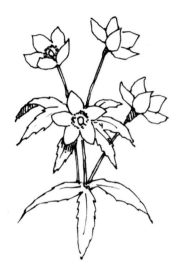

Christmas roses are members of the buttercup family and they do not do well in hot or warm winter climates, but are sensational in colder areas. The flowers are white and waxy-looking and they bloom roughly from November to April, but this varies in different areas. When cut, flowers last for about two weeks. Plants grow just under a foot high and do not bloom for two or three years after they are planted. The shiny, dark leaves are evergreen and are poisonous if eaten.

Christmas roses are perennials and are temperamental, but they can be grown successfully if the following tips are observed:

- They must have sun in the winter and shade in the summer.
- They must be protected from strong winds.
- They must never be allowed to dry out.
- They must never be moved.

A rose is a rose is a rose

except when it is a

Christmas Rose.

Planting
- Plant in the early spring or anytime until the frosts come.
- Plant a foot apart in a loamy soil with lots of leaf mold. They like the same soil as ferns.

Care
- Keep moist at all times, and water heavily on warm, summer days.
- Feed with a well-balanced fertilizer in the spring and in the summer when new growth appears.
- When cutting flowers for arrangements, sear or boil the ends of the stems.

CINERARIA

Senecio hybridus

The Big Yellow Tractor

Mike was only ten when it happened. He was sitting next to his father in a big yellow tractor. It had been raining heavily for days, and the soil had turned into a dark-brown, slushy mess.

No one knows for sure how it happened, but the tractor slid down a hill and fell over. Mike was not thrown clear. He lost a leg and an arm.

After months in the hospital, Mike came home. He lay in his bed for days and refused to leave his room. Finally, his mother got him in a wheelchair and took him outside to the patio. It was early spring and the days were warm and mild. His mother had gone to the local nursery and filled the patio with masses of blooming cinerarias. A weak smile formed on Mike's face when he looked at the beautiful flowers with such bright, vivid colors. The magnificent flowers cheered him up so much, he was soon out of his wheelchair and walking on his new leg. He is now a very successful lawyer, and every late winter and spring his own patio is filled with many colorful cinerarias.

CINERARIA

Cinerarias are perennials, but are usually treated as annuals. They hate cold and hot weather, and thrive in cool, shady spots. In mild climates, they bloom in late winter or early spring, and in cooler climates, they bloom in the spring and early summer.

The most popular cinerarias are the dwarf varieties called Multiflora Nana and Hybrida Grandiflora. These are compact plants that grow about a foot high. They have many clusters of large, daisy-like flowers in various strong shades of red, purple, blue, and white. Some have eyes and bands of another color. All varieties make excellent potted plants.

Planting
- In cold climates, plant young plants in the early spring. In mild climates, plant in the late fall or January.
- Mix leaf mold with the soil before planting, and be sure there is good drainage.
- Plant in the shade. They do well under trees.
- Plant 12" apart for solid color and further apart for a looser effect.

Care
- Protect plants from possible frosts.
- Plants must be kept moist, but do not let soil get soggy.
- Feed regularly with a well-balanced fertilizer or a fish emulsion.
- Watch for snails, slugs, aphids, whiteflies, and spider mites.
- In mild climates, plants will self-sow if they are in the right spot and have the proper care.
- After blooming, cut off the dead flowers. Shoots will start growing from the stems, and when they are strong, they can be cut off and rooted in sand or other rooting material.

CLIVIA, KAFFIR LILY
Clivia miniata

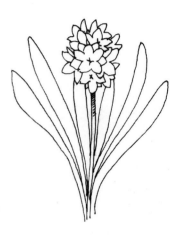

If you live in a mild or hot climate and want color in a dark spot in the garden, plant clivia. In cold climates, plants must be in pots and brought inside before the frosts arrive.

Clivias are perennials with tuberous roots. The handsome leaves are green the year round. Plants grow in large clumps and the flowers are in clusters. They bloom from December to April or from March to April, depending upon the area. Bright red berries appear after the blooming period. Plants look elegant massed under large trees or shrubs, and both the flowers and leaves make striking floral arrangements.

Planting

- Plants are sold at nurseries in gallon cans. The early fall or spring is a good time for planting in warm climates.
- Plant in a rich, moist soil but not an acid one.
- Plant in partial shade with the top of the tubers just above the soil level.

Care
- Feed regularly except during the blooming season.
- Tubers multiply into clumps and need to be divided every four or more years. Plants do not like to be disturbed so divide only when necessary. Do this in the spring after the blooming period.
- Keep plants well watered, but water sparingly when they are resting after the blooming period.
- Mealybugs often attack the leaves. Spray with Malathion or wash leaves with soapy water.

"Shed no tear -

O shed no tear!

The flower will bloom

another year."

John Keats

COCKSCOMB, CHINESE WOOLFLOWER *Celosia argentea*

Cockscombs are bizarre and flamboyant with wild disco colors that violently clash with anything near them. They have a soft, velvety texture and have much in common with the pregnancy of an elephant as they bloom a very long time. Cockscombs are grown in many gardens in Central America where vibrant colors are favored. They are dramatic annuals that love hot summers. Plants grow 2'-3' high. Dwarf varieties 10"-1' high.

There are two distinct varieties of cockscombs: the *Celosia cristata* (Crested) and the *Celosia plumosa* (Plumed). Crested flowers are shaped like ruffled combs on roosters (hence the common name), and the colors are gaudy shades of magenta, yellow, orange, maroon, and purple. The plumed varieties have clusters of flowers of deep crimson, gold, bright pink, and tangerine-red.

Planting
- Plant in the spring in full sun. Plants are available in flats.
- Plant 1' apart. Best when planted alone in groups of the same color.
- Not particular about soil, but plants do better in a rich one.

Cockscombs stand out in a garden like a lush at a Baptist picnic or a fille de joie at a meeting of the local Garden Club.

Care
- They are very easy to grow and need little care.

Things My Mother Never Told Me
- For a zingy, spectacular effect, plant cockscombs in the back of a bed with medium sized zinnias and dahlias in the foreground.
- Dry the blooms for winter bouquets.

COLEUS

Coleus hybridus or Coleus blumei

Coleuses are perennials but are treated like annuals. The luxurious leaves are strangely beautiful in wild combinations of many shades of green, salmon, shocking pink, chartreuse, orange, yellow, brown, wine-red, maroon, rust and purple. They look like they might have come from the Land of Oz.

Plants love the shade, and their eccentric colors brighten dark spots in the garden. They are originally from the tropics and hate cold weather. They make excellent house plants. There are large-leafed strains that grow 2'-3' high and dwarf varieties 1' high.

Planting
- Plant in the spring in partial shade. They wilt in full sun.
- Plant young plants from the nursery 12" apart in a soil with good drainage.

Care
- Pinch back when plants are about 6" high, and again when plants start to get leggy. They look best if kept just under 2'.
- To develop sturdy leaves, feed regularly with a fish emulsion or a fertilizer high in nitrogen. Never use a high bloom fertilizer as this will develop flowers.
- Plants like lots of water. Do not let soil dry out. In hot weather, mist or spray with water to keep them from drooping.
- Remove the tassel-like, blue flowers when they first develop. If they are not removed, flowers will go to seed and plants will stop growing.
- Coleuses are easy to propagate from cuttings, and will root in water.

Coleuses are like

rhubarb pie, figs,

abstract expressionism, and

chamber music - either you

like them or you

hate them.

COLUMBINE

Aquilegia

Columbine is an old favorite in the garden. The flowers with long spurs resemble tiny rockets blasting off to explore the cosmos. The blooms have many color combinations of soft pastels, red, blue, yellow, and white. They bloom in the spring and early summer. Some varieties have large flowers and long spurs and others have double flowers and short spurs.

Many species are native to various sections of the world. The Rocky Mountain Columbine is the state flower of Colorado, and a European species (*Aquilegia vulgaris*) has been naturalized in the East. A multitude of hybrids have been developed. All columbine plants are hardy. The tall ones grow 2'-3' high and the dwarf varieties grow about a foot high. Plants should be replaced every three or four years. They easily self-sow.

Planting

- In mild climates, plant in the spring or fall. In cold climates plant in the early spring after the frosts.
- Plant in partial shade. Can be in full sun in coastal areas.
- Plant in a sheltered place as plants are fragile and strong winds can destroy them.
- Plant 18" apart in a rich soil with good drainage.

"I've got spurs that

jingle, jangle, jingle"

Words from a popular song

Care

- Keep plants moist and feed regularly with a well-balanced fertilizer.
- When flowers fade, cut back to within 4" of the ground. New shoots will soon appear and flowers will bloom again. Cut back again after the second bloom.

CORAL BELLS

Heuchera sanguinea

These are dainty, yet hardy plants with a fairy-like quality. They could easily be Tinkerbell's favorite. They are perennials with clusters of tiny, bell-shaped flowers in shades of coral, pink, crimson and white. The leaves are heart-shaped and plants grow in low clumps. Coral Bells are excellent for ground covers and borders, and also for adding a whimsical touch to the garden. The graceful flowers are on slender stems 15"-24" high. They bloom from June to September in colder climates, and from April to August in milder ones. Plants multiply rapidly and the flowers are good for cutting. Some sturdy varieties are: 'June Bride' with pure white flowers, 'Matin Bells' with coral-red flowers, and 'Chatterbox' with rose-pink flowers. All of these are available at Wayside Gardens, Hodges, South Carolina, 29695.

Planting
- Plant in the fall or early spring in mild and hot areas, and in the early spring in cold areas.
- Plant a foot apart in the sun. In hot areas plant in partial shade.
- Plant in a loamy, well-drained soil.

Care
- Water frequently, and in the spring feed with a well-balanced fertilizer.
- Cut off all flowers at the end of the blooming season.
- Divide clumps every three or four years when they get crowded. In mild and hot areas, do this in the fall or spring, and in cold areas, divide them in the spring only. Keep the young, strong clumps and throw away the woody ones.

"She'll have rings

on her fingers

and bells on her toes."

From an old song

COREOPSIS, CALLIOPSIS

Coreopsis grandiflora &
Coreopsis tinctoria

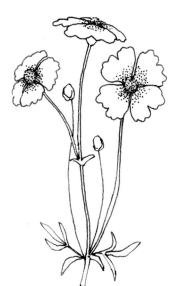

Coreopsis is one of the happiest and cheeriest flowers there is and it makes a great bedding plant. There are perennial and annual species. All are hardy, colorful, easy to grow, and often self-sow. Coreopsis resembles cosmos in shape and habits.

The perennial Coreopsis (*C. grandiflora*) grows 1'-2' high. The large yellow flowers are on long stems and bloom all summer. These plants are easily naturalized.

The annual Coreopsis (*C. tinctoria*) grows from 1'-3' high. There are also dwarf varities. Flowers are golden yellow, orange, crimson-brown, and bronze with brownish-purple centers. There are single and double ones and they are often bicolored. Flowers bloom from late spring to fall.

Planting

- Plants are easy to grow from seeds sown directly in the ground. Young plants are also available at nurseries.
- Sow seeds and plant young plants in full sun in the early spring 8"-12" apart.
- Not particular about type of soil.

Coreopsis is the Rebecca of

Sunnybrook Farm

and the Pollyanna

of the garden.

Care

- Plants practically raise themselves.
- Do not overwater. Can withstand droughts.
- Pick faded flowers to prolong blooming period.
- Stake plants if needed. Strong winds will harm them as the flower stems are very fragile.
- Occasionally feed with a well-balanced fertilizer.
- Divide perennials when needed in early spring.

COSMOS

Cosmos bipinnatus

Cosmos were very popular during the Victorian era, but they fell out of grace a few decades ago. They should be rediscovered as they are easy to grow and give a charming, old-fashioned touch to a garden.

Plants are fast growing annuals that require little care and are drought resistant. The leaves are lacy and graceful, and the flowers bloom in the summer and early fall. They are single, double, frilled or crested in beautiful shades of pink, purple, red, and white. There are many different varieties that grow from 3'-8' high. Plants from the new Sensation strain are not quite as tall as the older species and they bloom earlier. There is also a Yellow Cosmos (*C. sulphureus*).

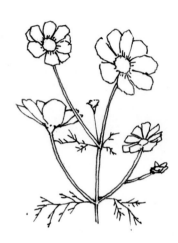

Planting
- Seeds can be sown directly in the ground any time in the spring or early summer. Young plants are available at nurseries in the spring.
- Plant in full sun 10" apart at the back of a bed as these are tall plants.
- Will grow in almost any soil except a soggy and a very rich one.

Care
- Pinch back plants when they are about 6" high to make them bushier.
- Feed regularly with a well-balanced fertilizer.
- Stake plants to help support their fragile stems.
- Cosmos easily reseed themselves. In mild climates, the supply of plants should more than double the following spring.

The person

unable to grow cosmos

"should of stood in bed."

Thanks to Casey Stengel

Things My Mother Never Told Me
- Plunge cosmos flowers in cool water as soon as possible after cutting as they are very delicate and will quickly wilt.

CROCUS, DUTCH CROCUS
Crocus vernus

A Modern Day Rip Van Winkle

It was January and the sky, trees, houses, and streets were all a monotonous, dreary gray. Howling winds were breaking off small limbs from the bare trees and everything looked malformed and eerie. In one of the houses, a young boy with curly, blond hair lay sprawled on the floor in front of a glowing fire of eucalyptus logs. A calico cat and a large brown dog lay beside him. They all were enjoying the warmth of the fire. Loud rock music blasted forth from the stereo. In spite of the cacophony, everyone was sound asleep. In a corner a small blue and white ceramic pot filled with eight unopened crocus buds sat on a table, whose polished surface reflected the dancing light from the fire.

The music reached a crescendo, and four of the crocus buds burst into full bloom. The three prone figures stirred. The dog scratched, the cat stretched, and the boy sat up. Then he saw the blooming crocus and shouted, "Ye gads! I've slept through the winter. It's spring and the crocuses are blooming!"

How wrong he was. Some crocuses bloom when the days are blustery and cold and the winds are fiercely blowing.

CROCUS, DUTCH CROCUS

Crocuses are corms, and there are many different species. This one is the most vigorous and popular. It thrives in cold climates, but will grow in mild areas, and is the species used for forced blooming in pots. Plants are 3" high and make a spectacular ground cover. Flowers are purple, lavender, yellow, and white. Some have stripes and are feathered. They bloom in late January through March, depending upon the area. There are other species that bloom in the spring and in the fall.

Planting
- Crocus corms are sold at nurseries in the fall. They can also be ordered from growers who specialize in bulbs.
- Plant in full sun or semi-shade. Because plants are small they should be massed in groups. They can also be planted between bricks and stepping stones, in a rock garden, or naturalized in a lawn. Plant 2"-3" deep in a porous soil.

Care
- Corms will multiply if left in the ground. Divide them every three or four years.
- If planted in pots, they can be left in the pots or dug up and stored in a dry place until the following fall.

Things My Mother Never Told Me
- To make saffron, dry the stigmas of crocus and remove the pollen.

CYCLAMEN, FLORISTS' CYCLAMEN   *Cyclamen persicum*

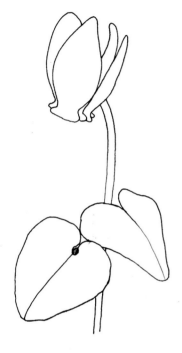

A few years ago I bought forty young cyclamen plants because I wanted to learn all their idiosyncrasies. I ended with three survivors. The most important fact I learned is that these plants must be kept moist, but they will rot away like pollywog tails if given too much water.

Cyclamen are tuberous perennials and plants in this species are temperamental and difficult. They hate cold weather and are extremely sensitive to changes in temperatures. Potted plants will wither if left in a hot room over a period of a few days. The graceful flowers are white and many different shades of glorious reds from a pale, soft pink to a deep crimson. They bloom in the late fall until spring.

There are many other species of cyclamen. Some are hardier and have smaller flowers. These are usually used as ground covers or naturalized under trees.

Planting
- The best time for planting most species is during the summer when the tubers are dormant. Sprouted tubers are available at many nurseries in the late fall.
- Plant 6"-10" apart in partial shade with at least half the tuber above the soil. Plant other species 1/2" deep.
- Plant in a rich soil that has good drainage.

Care
- Keep plants constantly moist, but never soggy.
- Watch for bugs and feed regularly.
- Pick off dead flowers before pods form.
- Cyclamen die back after blooming and become dormant. Do not feed at this time and water very sparingly. Begin to water regularly when new shoots appear in the early fall.
- In cold climates bring potted plants inside before the frosts come and keep them in the coolest room in the house.

If you want a real challenge

like swimming the

Hellespont, landing a

1,000 pound marlin, or

hailing a taxi during a rain

storm, try growing

cyclamen in pots.

CYMBIDIUM

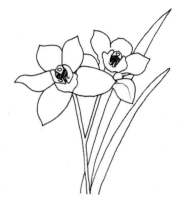

Terrestrial Orchids

Cymbidium flowers are outrageously exotic and they bloom for at least a month. Plants are easy to grow in mild climates and require little care. In cold climates they must be brought inside or placed in a greenhouse for the winter. People who do not grow cymbidiums, and who live in areas where they can be grown, are "airheads", a favorite expression of my eleven-year-old grandson.

Cymbidiums are pseudo-bulbs. They are most successfully grown out-doors in pots. When plants bloom, the pots can be brought inside for display or the spikes of flowers can be cut and placed in vases. More than a dozen flowers are often on one stem. Most plants bloom any-where from February until the end of May. A few bloom in December. There are many large and small flowered varieties of hybrids in a wide range of colors.

Planting

- The amount of sunlight a plant gets is very important for good blooms. They should be in a spot where plants will get enough sunlight so that the foliage is a greenish-yellow color. If leaves are a deep green, the plant is in too much shade. Not enough sunlight is usually the reason why plants do not bloom. They do well in filtered sunlight beneath trees. Do not place them in full sun.
- Plant in a rich, slightly acid soil that has good drainage. A good mixture is: 2 parts redwood chips or fir bark; 2 parts peat moss, and 1 part sand or perlite. There are many good packaged cymbidium soil mixes.

CYMBIDIUM

Care
- When plants are in their growing season, roughly from March to October, keep the soil on the moist side, but never let it get soggy. The tips of the leaves might die back if the soil is allowed to dry out at this time.
- On hot days, spray foliage with water early or late in the day.
- From July to January feed every two weeks with a high-bloom (6-30-30) fertilizer. From January to July with a 30-10-10 one.
- Watch for snails and slugs. Generously sprinkle snail bait all around the plants when flower spikes first appear.

Dividing Cymbidium Plants
- Only divide or repot plants when there is no more room for new bulbs to grow. They like to be crowded.
- If plants have not bloomed, divide in March. If they have bloomed, divide as soon as the flowers fade. If divided after July 1, they will probably not bloom the following year.
- Always keep at least 3-5 bulbs in a division.
- After dividing plants, wash or shake off as much soil as possible and remove any dead roots. If possible, pull bulbs apart. Some times a sterile knife must be used to separate them.
- Spread out the roots. Work soil in and around them and water lightly to settle the soil. Keep newly potted plants in a well shaded spot and do not overwater. When roots begin to grow, place them in a less shady spot and begin their regular, normal care.

DAHLIA

Modern dahlias are hybrids and are tuberous perennials that grow from 1'-6' high. There are about 2,000 varieties. The miniatures, dwarfs, and pompons are used as borders or in pots and planters. The larger varieties are planted in beds or in cutting gardens, and the dinner-plate size varieties are for exhibitions or to dazzle the neighbors. Flowers bloom in summer and have many different shapes and sizes and are almost every color but blue.

Planting
- Plant tubers in the spring in full sun in a loamy soil.
- Put a small amount of superphosphate at the bottom of each planting hole. Place tubers horizontally with the eye or sprouts facing up. Small dahlias should be 1'-2' apart and large ones 3'-4' apart. Cover hole with 3" of soil.
- Place a 5' stake in the planting hole of the tall varieties for support. Face the eye of the tuber toward the stake.

Dahlia petals are

recurved, incurved,

collared, or quilled.

Care
- Keep well watered when plants begin to grow.
- Pinch back plants when they are 12"-18" high. On tall varieties, leave 2-4 of the strongest stalks and pinch off the others.
- For large flowers, remove all buds except those on the tips.
- Use a well-balanced fertilizer every two weeks.
- When cutting flowers for arrangements, sear the ends of the stems by putting them in boiling water or burning them over a stove.
- In cold climates in the fall when the stalks have turned yellow, dig up the tubers and dry them in the sun for a few hours, store in a cool, dry place for the winter. In mild climates tubers can be left in the ground where they will multiply.
- Tubers can be divided before storing or just before planting in the spring. When dividing be sure to leave 1" of stalk with an eye attached to each tuber. Tubers without an eye will not grow.

DAYLILY

Hemerocallis

Daylilies are not members of the lily family. They belong to an entirely different genus called *Hemerocallis*. They are hardy perennials that are easy to grow and can withstand the heat and dry weather better than most flowers. There are early, mid-season, and late bloomers. With proper planning, you can have daylilies blooming from May to October. Insects and pests practically never bother them. Plants grow 1'-6' high.

There are many colors. Some are various shades of pink, peach, purple, and near white. Some are bi-colored and multicolored. Flowers are single, semi-double, and double.

Planting
- In colder climates, the best time for planting is in the spring. In mild climates plant anytime.
- Plant in full sun. In hot climates, plant in partial shade. They will not bloom if they do not get enough sun.
- Daylilies are an informal plant, and they get untidy at certain times of the year. They are spectacular when naturalized.
- Not particular about type of soil, but will do best if soil has been well prepared and has good drainage.
- Plant 2'-3' apart with the crowns at soil level. Some gardeners prefer the crowns to be 1" above the soil.

Care
- Water plants well during the growing and blooming season.
- Feed with a complete fertilizer in the spring and mid-summer.
- In the fall or early spring, divide clumps that have become crowded. Usually this is done every four or five years. Each section should have a crown bud and strong roots. Leave some of the clump intact because the new sections will not bloom well - if at all - the first year after replanting.

A few brand names of daylilies are 'Far Out', 'Turned On', 'Mama Cha Cha', and 'Chicago Blackout'.

DELPHINIUM, CANDLE LARKSPUR
Delphinium elatum

Delphiniums are dramatic plants that are basically native to cool climates and high altitudes, but they excel and thrive on the Pacific Coast and in New England. In the midwest or in any other hot area away from the coast, they are temperamental and difficult. They are perennials but are often treated as annuals. Annual delphiniums or larkspurs belong to another genus (*Consolida ambigua*).

The tallest and grandest delphiniums are the Pacific Hybrids or the Pacific Giants. Dwarf Giant Pacific strain plants are 2' high. Flowers are various subtle shades of blue, white, pink, and lavender. Some have "bees" or centers of a different color. In mild climates they bloom in late spring and early summer. In cold climates in summer and early fall.

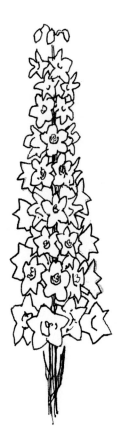

Planting
- Plant young plants in early spring. In mild areas can also be planted in fall.
- Plant in full sun in a soil which is on the alkaline side and has good drainage.
- Put a pinch of bonemeal at bottom of planting holes. Do not cover root crowns with soil.
- Plant 1'-2' apart. They look spectacular planted along a fence or as a background in a border. Plants must have good air circulation.

Delphiniums are as

Care

majestic as the mighty

- Feed regularly with a balanced fertilizer, and watch for snails and slugs.
- Stake plants before they need it.

Rockies and as regal as

- When weather is warm, keep plants well watered and put mulch on soil to keep roots cool.

King John signing the

- Cut faded flowers after they have bloomed. When new shoots begin to grow and are several inches high, cut off all old stalks. In mild climates, plants should bloom again.

Magna Charta.

DIANTHUS, PINK, COTTAGE PINK
Dianthus plumarius

Who is Rhett Butler?

Recently I went to a wedding, and most of the guests were born in the Fifties. The young ushers wore shirts with many ruffles. I had known them since they had progressed from scooters, tricycles, skateboards, to secondhand automobiles. I said to one usher, "You look just like Rhett Butler!" He stared at me and replied, "Who is Rhett Butler?"

I was as stunned as my Old Gardening Friend with the High Rubber Boots must have been years ago when he asked me, "How is your dianthus?" I replied in an icy voice, "I don't know what you are talking about." He broke into a huge belly laugh and informed me that dianthus is the generic name for a large group of plants, which includes carnations, sweet williams, and many species of pinks.

Pinks or dianthus are low growing perennials with flower stems 5"-18" high. Flowers are single or double with a spicy fragrance and bloom profusely from early summer to the middle of fall. Colors are shades of red, pink, purple, and white with dark centers.

Planting
- In mild climates, plant young plants in fall or spring. In cold climates, in spring.
- Plant in full sun, or partial shade in hot climates.
- Plant in a rich soil with good drainage. Plants hate an acid soil.

Care
- Feed regularly with a well-balanced fertilizer.
- The more flowers you cut, the more blooms you will get.
- In mild climates, cut plants back to about 4" after blooming.

DUSTY MILLER

Senecio cineraria &
Centaurea cineraria

Dusty Miller is a name that is loosely given to many plants that have woolly, gray-white, velvety leaves. *Senecio cineraria* and *Centaurea cineraria* are two of the most familiar species, and they are so similar they are being discussed in the same chapter. Both genera have compact plants, and both are perennials that are very easy to grow and require little care. *C. cineraria* has small single, purple or yellow flowers in the summer. These plants are 1'-1 1/2' high. *S. cineraria* has small clusters of yellow flowers, and in mild climates they bloom almost the year round. Plants are about 2' high.

Dusty Millers are the arbitrators and peacemakers in the garden because their gray-white leaves neutralize clashing colors. The French are well aware of this virtue, and almost every garden in France has some of these plants. They also make excellent borders.

Dusty Miller is as common a name in the flower world as Smith or Jones is in the real world.

Planting
- In mild climates plant in spring or fall, and in cold climates, plant in the spring.
- Plant in full sun. Not too particular about type of soil, but does not like an acid one.

Care
- Pinch back young plants to make them bushier.
- Do not overwater, as they dislike a soil that is too moist.
- Feed occasionally with a well-balanced fertilizer.
- Trim plants after they have bloomed if they are straggly.
- Cuttings can be made in the summer.

ENGLISH DAISY
Bellis perennis

There are French perfumes, German beers, Scotch whiskies, Irish tweeds, Italian pastas, and English daisies. The later are small plants whose ancestors were found growing in meadows.

English daisies are perennials that hate hot weather and are treated as annuals in many areas. Numerous new varieties have been developed with double flowers. In cold climates flowers bloom in spring and early summer, and in mild climates, they bloom in late winter. Flowers are red, pink, crimson, and white, and are single or double. Plants grow 6"-8" high. They are charming when naturalized in lawns, or tucked among other flowers in a bed. They also make a good border or a ground cover for bulbs.

Planting
- In the spring, plant young plants 5" apart.
- Plant in partial shade in warm climates, and in full sun in coastal areas.
- Not particular about type of soil.

"Speak gently,

she can hear the

daisies grow."

Oscar Wilde

Care
- Keep soil moist but not soggy.
- Feed occasionally with a well-balanced fertilizer.
- Divide plants after they have bloomed if the clumps become crowded.
- Plants will self-sow if they are in the right environment and double flowers will eventually go back to their original single flower.

FELICIA, BLUE MARGUERITE
Felicia amelloides

In Spanish, felicidad means happy, and felicidad and felicia are practically synonymous. This is indeed a happy, cheery plant. It is one of my favorites because it is so prolific and is as rugged as Mt. Everest.

Felicias are perennials that grow about 18" high. In cold climates they are treated as annuals. Plants spread rapidly and self-sow. The leaves are evergreen and the winsome flowers resemble small, blue daisies. In mild climates they bloom almost continuously if the dead flowers are removed. Plants are often used as ground covers, and they are excellent in pots and hanging baskets. In cold climates felicias must be grown in pots and brought inside for the winter.

Planting
- In cold climates plant young plants in the spring. In mild climates can be planted in the fall or spring.
- Plants prefer full sun, but can be in partial shade.
- Not particular about the soil.

Care
- Do not overwater.
- Pick off dead flowers for profuse blooms. I sit in luxury on a small stool while doing this because it is a tedious, time-consuming job.
- Plants become leggy and woody if they are not trimmed. In the late summer, severely cut back plants to 4"-5" high.
- Cuttings can be made from side shoots in the fall or early spring.

FEVERFEW

Chrysanthemum parthenium

The Ding-Dong-Daddy of the D Car Line

In San Francisco quite a few years ago, a man was arrested for having seven wives at the same time. He was a streetcar conductor, and the *San Francisco Chronicle* referred to him as the Ding-Dong-Daddy of the D Car Line. The feverfew plant reminds me of this latter-day Casanova because it springs up all over the garden and is a self-sower of seeds.

These plants are members of the chrysanthemum family and were great favorites with the Victorians. They are perennials and are covered with many small, daisy-like flowers that give a lavender-and-old-lace feeling to a garden. Some gardeners consider them weeds because they are so prolific. Plants are ideal for the lazy gardener as they even pop up between bricks in a patio and just grow and grow.

There are many varieties that vary in height from 1'-3' high. A popular one is 'Golden Feather'. It has lacy chartreuse leaves and white flowers with yellow centers. They are great in floral arrangements.

Planting
- In cold climates plant in spring. In other climates can be planted the year round.
- Will grow in full sun or semi shade.
- Not particular about type of soil. New plants that spring up can be transplanted, left where they are, or put in pots to be given to friends. Cuttings can also be made, but why bother?

Care
- Plants require little or no care. Just water them and watch them grow.

FORGET-ME-NOT
Myosotis sylvatica

Hopefully, forget-me-nots will return to popularity because they are delicate looking flowers that are hardy and easy to grow. They need very little care, and the tiny flowers add a touch of fantasy to a garden and to a bouquet. Plants like lots of moisture and partial shade.

They are annuals or biennials and grow 6"-12" high and bloom in late winter or early spring. They readily reseed themselves and often take over a flower bed.

There is a perennial forget-me-not (*Myosotis scorpioides*) that spreads by creeping roots and is often used as a ground cover or in hanging baskets. The summer, or cape forget-me-not, belongs to an entirely different genus (*Anchusa capensis*). These plants grow 1 1/2'-2' high and are annual and biennial. The pure blue flowers bloom in the summer.

Planting
- In mild climates, plant young plants in the spring or fall. In cold climates, plant in the spring.
- Plant in partial shade 6" apart in soil with lots of organic matter.

Care
- Keep plants well watered, and feed regularly with a well-balanced fertilizer.
- After blooming, cut plants back to about 6" high. They will grow and bloom again.
- Plants can be divided and cuttings can be made.

Once airedales were popular. Springer spaniels, golden retrievers, and labradors are in vogue now. Forget-me-nots have been out of style about as long as airedales.

FOUR O'CLOCK, MARVEL OF PERU
Mirabilis jalapa

In The Ancient City Of Chan Chan

Many years before anyone had heard of Pizarro, a young maiden named Marvel lived in the ancient city of Chan Chan on the coastal desert of Northern Peru. Marvel labored all day in the maize fields. The sun was scorching hot and the work was hard. One day she went to the great Chimor monarch and told him the rays of the sun were spoiling her beautiful skin. She wanted to sleep during the day and work in the evenings. The mighty monarch brewed a concoction of snake scales and bat guano. When Marvel drank it, she turned into a beautiful flower. This flower does not bloom when the skies are sunny. It comes out around four o'clock. You guessed it! The name of the flower is Four o'clock or Marvel of Peru.

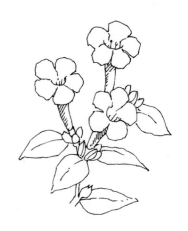

These plants should hire

a public relations firm to

let people know how great

they are.

Four o'clocks are easy to grow and are fast growers. The flowers fold up in the bright sunlight and start blooming when the sun is low on the horizon. The French call this colorful plant "Belle de Nuit". They are perennials, but in cold climates, they are treated as annuals. The roots are tuberous and the plants grow in wide clumps 3'-4' high. The many branches of flowers have a faint lemon fragrance and are red, white, and yellow. They bloom from the middle of summer until the frosts and readily reseed themselves.

Planting
- Many nurseries do not stock the tuberous roots, but seeds can be sown right in the ground after the frosts.
- Plants like a sunny location but will grow in partial shade.
- Plant 1' - 2' apart.
- Not particular about type of soil, but drainage should be good.

Care
- Keep plants well watered.
- In cold climates, the tuberous roots can be dug up and stored until the next spring.

FOXGLOVE, DIGITALIS
Digitalis purpurea

Foxglove is an old favorite with gardeners. Other names for it could be Bells of St. Mary or Temple Bells. The beautiful spikes of tubular-shaped flowers resemble tall spires on Gothic cathedrals or on the temples at Angkor Wat. In England these plants grow wild along many shady, country roads.

The plants are biennial and occasionally perennial. They grow 2'-6' high, and the leaves are light-green and woolly. The drug, digitalis, comes from them. Flowers are on spikes 1'-2' long and many are spotted. They bloom in the late spring to early fall and there are colors of purple, yellow, pink, crimson, and white. Hummingbirds love their nectar. Some popular varieties are 'Foxy' (3'), and 'Giant Shirley' (6')

Planting

- In mild climates, plant young plants in the fall. In colder climates in the spring.
- Plant in partial shade. In coastal areas, they can be in full sun.
- Plant 2' apart at the back of a shady bed or naturalize them among shrubs, ferns, or under trees.
- Not particular about type of soil, but prefers a moist soil that is on the acid side.

Care

- Keep plants moist and feed regularly with a well-balanced fertilizer.
- Watch for snails, slugs, and aphids.
- After the first bloom, cut the flowers and side shoots will develop. Plants will bloom again and will reseed themselves.
- Plants grown from seed will not bloom the first year. In shady places, plants will naturalize and are often white.

FREESIA

Freesia hybrid

Freesias are native to South Africa and are most successfully grown in mild areas such as California where they are grown commercially for florists. In cold climates they must be grown indoors, and they will fill a room with an ambrosial fragrance.

Freesias are corms, and when planted outdoors, they come up forever more. The tubular flowers bloom in the early spring and grow on branched 1'-1 1/2' slender stems. Old varieties are white or a creamy white. There are many new Dutch hybrids and Tecolote varieties whose flowers come in as many colors as there are in Joseph's coat or in a painting by Jackson Pollock.

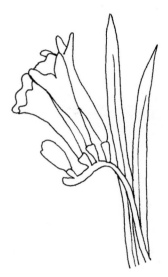

Planting
- Plant anytime from September to December in full sun.
- Plant in a soil with good drainage.
- Place the pointed end of the corms up and plant 2" deep and 2" apart. When plants are close together, they help hold each other up.

"There can be no perfect

flower without fragrance."

Stéphane Mallarmé

Care
- Keep well watered when the weather is hot.
- Feed regularly with a balanced fertilizer and stake if necessary.
- Leave corms in the ground after blooming and let plants die back before removing foliage.
- Divide clumps about every three or four years.

FUCHSIA

Fuchsia hybrida

It Was a Magnificent Performance

Fuchsias are the ballet dancers of the flower world. They wear beautiful tutus and leotards that are the colors of a spectacular sunset. In the summer when a gentle breeze blows, they do a slow and graceful dance. If it is windy, they do 'grand jetes en tournant'. Last night after three martinis - very dry - I saw Nureyev and Fonteyn dance "Swan Lake" in a pot which was suspended from an umbrella in my patio. She was dressed in shades of the palest pinks, and he wore a deep salmon tunic with leotards the color of orange drops. Nijinsky watched from a redwood box which was hanging from an arbor covered with scarlet bougainvillea. He had on a deep purple robe. The Wise Old Owl sat enthralled in his Ginkgo Tree, and uninvited snails, slugs, and cutworms surreptitiously watched from a slimy rock at the bottom of the garden. It was a magnificent performance.

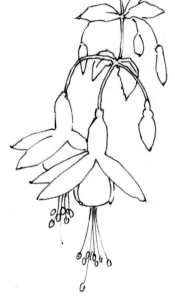

Fuchsias are very particular about their environment. They must have moisture, and they thrive on foggy coasts where the temperature is mild and the sun shines for at least part of the day. Forget them if you live in areas where the summers are hot and dry. In cold climates, they must be grown in pots and brought inside for the winter. Plants are perennials and grow erect to 3'-14' high and many trail. The erect ones are used as shrubs or in pots and planters. They can also be trained into small trees. The trailing ones are used in hanging baskets.

There are hundreds of varieties. The flowers have many color combinations in various shades of purple, pink, red, salmon, and white. They are single, double, ruffled, or elongated, and their size varies from small to the size of ranunculus.

FUCHSIA

Planting
- Buy young plants or make cuttings from old ones in the early spring. See Chapter Fourteen, "How to Beat Inflation by Propagation."
- Plant in filtered light. They hate the midday sun.
- Add coarse sand, peat moss, or ground bark to soil as plants must have good drainage. Also add these to a regular planting or potting mix if they are being used.

Care
- Water fuchsias often. Never let the soil dry out or become soggy.
- Mist plants with a fine spray of water in hot weather.
- Feed with a complete fertilizer about every two weeks during the growing season.
- Pick off dead flowers to keep berries from forming. These slow down the blooming period.
- Severely cut back plants once a year. There is a great difference of opinion as to the proper time to do this. In mild climates, one expert says November and another one says January or February. Potted plants are cut back to almost the edge of the pots, and plants in the ground are cut back to about half their size. In cold climates, slightly prune plants when they are brought inside for the winter, and severely prune them in the spring after the frosts.
- After pruning, stop feeding until new growth appears.
- When new growth has three leaves, pinch off the tip. When the new growth from the pinch has three leaves, pinch their tips off. If a plant was pruned in November, keep pinching until March, and later if pruned in the early spring. A good rule of thumb is to keep pinching until a plant is well-shaped and bushy. If a plant becomes leggy in the summer, pinch it back once more.

GARDENIA, CAPE JASMINE
Gardenia jasminoides

"Long ago and far away" is a strain from a favorite Glenn Miller song, and when he played it long ago, practically every girl on the ballroom floor had a white gardenia in her hair. Hopefully, someday this charming tradition will be revived.

Gardenia plants are evergreen shrubs with many fragrant, white blossoms. Unfortunately, they will not grow in cold climates, but they thrive and are easy to grow in warm ones. Plants must have hot summers to grow and bloom well. Different varieties grow 2'-8' high, and they make a wonderfully fragrant hedge or background plant. They also are good tub plants.

Flowers are single or double. They bloom from May-July, and in some climates until October or November. 'Mystery' is one of the most popular of all varieties. It has large, double blooms and plants can grow to 8' high.

Planting
- Plant in the fall or spring.
- Can be planted in full sun along the coastal areas, and in partial shade in hotter climates.
- Likes an acid soil. Add peat moss or ground bark to soil before planting.
- Plant slightly above ground level, and do not crowd other plants around them.

GARDENIA

Care
- Plants require lots of water.
- Feed regularly during the growing season with a fertilizer formulated for gardenias (10-8-7) or one that is high in acids. A fish emulsion can also be used.
- If leaves turn yellow, give plants a dose of chelated iron.
- Do not cultivate around plants. They have very shallow roots. Mulch them instead with peat moss or ground bark.
- Remove all buds but one on each leaf axil. This will help produce larger and more fragrant flowers.
- If buds drop, it is probably due to too much humidity or overfeeding.
- When plants become straggly, prune them in spring before new growth starts.
- In cold climates, they can be grown in tubs and brought inside for the winter - inside a greenhouse, that is. If brought indoors, plants must have a humid atmosphere and a sunny location.

GERBERA DAISY, TRANSVAAL DAISY
Gerbera jamesonii

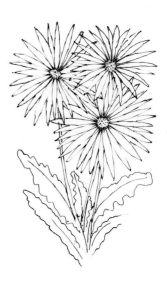

Gerberas are native to the Transvaal in South Africa, and add a lot of class to a garden because they are aristocratic and sophisticated. They are hardy perennials in mild climates, but must be brought inside where winters are cold. Plants have graceful leaves and grow in 10" high clumps.

Flowers bloom almost year round, but mostly in the summer. They are on leafless stems about 18" long and are excellent in arrangements. There are many hybrids with single, double, ruffled, bicolored, and duplex (two rows of petals) flowers. The colors are gorgeous shades of tangerine, coral, pink, yellow, cream, and red. For a spectacular show, mass different colors in one bed. They are also effective when planted in large pots or tubs.

Planting
- Young plants are available at nurseries from spring until fall. Buy them when they are in bloom so you know what color they are. Get all the various colors available or all you can afford. Plants are good investments because they multiply.
- Plant in full sun. In hot climates, plant in partial shade. Do not let soil cover the crowns.
- Plant in a loamy soil with good drainage 1'-2' apart with the crowns just above the soil.

Care
- They require lots of water. Flowers will droop if soil is permitted to dry out too much. Water deeply but do not let soil become soggy.
- Feed regularly with a well-balanced fertilizer.
- When clumps become crowded, divide them anytime from February to April.
- Keep old leaves and flowers picked and watch for snails.

There are many "trans".

A few are Trans-Siberian

Railroad, transcendental-

ism, transmogrify,

transvestite, and

transvaal daisies.

GLADIOLUS, GARDEN GLADIOLUS
Gladiolus hortulanus

Plants are corms, and the many hybrids have been divided into five groups - miniature, small, medium, large, and giant. They grow from 3'-5' high. Flowers are white, cream, salmon, yellow, rose, lavender, scarlet, many smoky colors, and brilliant shades of red and purple.

Planting
- In cold climates plant in April, May or June. In mild climates plant from November to March.
- Plant in full sun in a light, sandy soil with good drainage. In hot areas, plant in partial shade.
- The best corms have high crowns. Plant them four times their own depth. Place smaller corms 4" apart and the larger ones 6" apart.
- Stagger planting time for a longer blooming time.
- Plant in the back of a flower bed or in rows in cutting beds.

Care
- Fertilize regularly until buds bloom.
- Spray with Malathion if plants get thrips or spider mites.
- If corms are left in the ground after blooming, cut back plants to about one foot to prevent thrips. Remove leaves when they turn yellow.
- If corms are dug up and stored, dry them before pulling off the old corms and roots. Store the new corms and cormels in a dark, dry, well-ventilated place.

Ooh La La! Mais Oui!

In France practically all

restaurants, from small

country ones to the Tour

d'Argent, have at least one

large vase of tall gladiolus.

Things My Mother Never Told Me
- Cut gladiolus for arrangements when the lowest bud on the stalk begins to open.
- Cut flowers will last longer if bottoms of stems are slit about 1" or cut at an angle. This permits more water to reach the flowers.

GLORIOSA DAISY, BLACK-EYED SUSAN
Rudbeckia hirta

The Eliza Doolittle of America

Black-eyed Susan is the Eliza Doolittle of America. Eliza grew up in a tough section of London. Susan grew wild in the fields and pastures of the Eastern part of the USA. She was an ordinary, yellow daisy with a dark center. A horticulturist fell in love with her and turned Susan into a glamorous flower named Gloriosa Daisy. She now has double ruffles or single ones that are either yellow, orange, russet, mahogany, and yellow-banded with maroon.

The gloriosa daisy is a biennial, but is often grown as an annual. It grows 3'-4' high and one bush produces many flowers which bloom in the summer and early fall. The flowers are very cheery looking, and they brighten up the garden. They are also great for cutting.

Planting
- Sow seeds in early spring or plant young plants in late spring or early summer.
- Prefers full sun, but will grow in partial shade.
- Not particular about soil, but must have good drainage.
- Plant about a foot apart.

Care
- Feed regularly with a well-balanced fertilizer.
- Keep faded flowers picked.
- After the blooming season, cut stalks to the ground. This will encourage new growth.
- These plants readily self-sow, so there is a steady supply of new plants.

GLOXINIA

Sinningia speciosa

Gloxinias are tubers and are native to tropical forests. They thrive in an atmosphere that is warm and humid. They will not tolerate cold climates, but they make an excellent and colorful house plant or potted plant for the patio in the spring and summer. In mild climates, gloxinias can be planted in the garden, but they must be in a sheltered spot with filtered shade.

Flowers bloom in the late spring and summer. They are trumpet-shaped and have a velvety texture and are single or double. The colors are purple, violet, dark red, crimson, pink, white, and blue. Often they are marbled or spotted with darker shades. If cared for properly, one plant will produce many buds. Florists love these plants because they are so colorful and make an excellent gift.

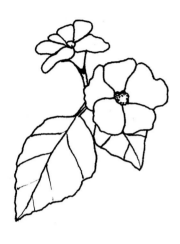

This plant is the W. C.

Fields of the flower world.

It likes to get potted.

Planting in Pots
- Tubers are available at nurseries, or they can be ordered by mail from growers who specialize in them. Plant them in January or February with the rounded part down. Place tubers 1" below the soil level.
- Plant large tubers in 7" or 8" pots and smaller ones in 6" or 7" ones. Keep in a warm spot with filtered sunlight. Tubers can also be started in flats and transferred to pots when a good root system develops.
- Soil should be rich. One expert recommends a soil that is 2 parts leaf mold, 1 part peat moss, and 1 part loam. The Wise Old Owl in the Ginkgo Tree is extravagant and uses the packaged soil for African violets.

GLOXINIA

Care

- When plants first start to grow, water sparingly. Never let water get on the leaves.
- If more than one sprout appears, break or cut off all but the main shoot.
- Increase the watering as leaves begin to grow. Keep the soil moist but never let it get soggy - or dry. For pots, use water that is at room temperature.
- During the growing period, feed every two or three weeks with a well-balanced fertilizer that has been diluted to one-half the recommended strength.
- If plant gets too much sun, the leaves will burn, and if not enough sunlight, the leaves will get large and there will be few flowers.
- Keep faded flowers picked, and keep plants away from drafts.
- When plants become dormant in the fall or winter, gradually withhold watering. When plants become withered, pull off foliage and store pots in a cool, dark spot. Some gardeners remove the tubers from the pots, cut off all roots, and store them in slightly moist peat moss.
- In January or February, new growth will begin to appear. Repot all tubers and don't forget to water sparingly at first. Flowers will not be so plentiful the second year.
- Gloxinias can be propagated by leaf cuttings. Root in sand, moist sphagnum moss, or other rooting material.

HOLLYHOCK

Alcea rosea &
Althaea rosea

A cottage in the English countryside isn't complete without a row of hollyhocks in the garden. The colonists brought them to America and Williamsburg had more hollyhocks than colonists. Now they are considered as old-fashioned as running boards and hip flasks. This is a crime as they are very stately and magnificent, and their masses of beautiful colors add glamour to a garden. They reseed themselves readily, and are often found growing wild by the side of a country lane.

Hollyhocks are biennial or short lived perennials. They are used as background plants in beds, and are often planted along a fence, wall, or trellis. There are many different varieties that grow from 4'-8' high, and the flowers are single or double on long spikes. They bloom in the summer and early fall and are soft shades of maroon, rose, yellow, salmon, white, red, and purple.

Why does a star shine?

Why did Rome fall?

Why are hollyhocks not

popular anymore?

Planting
- Plant young plants in early spring 2'-3' apart and low in the soil to give them a good base.
- Easy to raise from seed, which can be sown directly in the ground after the frosts.
- Not particular about soil, but must have good air circulation and sun.

Care
- Keep plants well watered, particularly when it is hot.
- Feed regularly with a well-balanced fertilizer.
- Plants are subject to rust. Spray with a bordeaux mixture before it attacks, or spray the undersides of the leaves with a fine sulphur dust in the early spring.
- Cut stalks to the ground after flowers have bloomed.

HYACINTH, DUTCH HYACINTH
Hyacinthus orientalis

Hyacinths are as fragrant as a bottle of Arpege and as formal as a State Dinner at the White House. They thrive outdoors in cold climates and rabbits don't eat the bulbs. The blooming period is early in the spring, and they are easy to grow indoors in containers.

Dutch hyacinths are bulbs of varying sizes. The largest ones are used for potting. Flowers are single or double and are pink, blue, creamy pastels, and deep shades of red, purple, yellow, blue, and pure white. There is a Roman or French Roman hyacinth (*H. orientalis albulus*). It does not have as many flowers per stem.

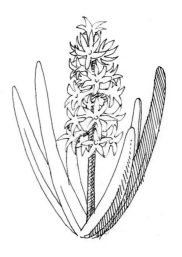

Planting
- In cold climates, plant in September-October before the ground freezes. In mild areas, plant in October-December.
- Plant in sun or partial shade in a rich soil with good drainage.
- Because plants are delicate they look better massed together.
- Plant bulbs 6" deep and 6" apart. This varies with the size of the bulb. Place sand and bonemeal at the bottom of each hole.

Planting in Pots
- Use a potting soil with good drainage, and set bulbs so the tops are close to the surface of the soil.
- Place pots in a dark spot until a good root system is formed, which will be in about six or eight weeks. Then bring them gradually into the sunlight.
- Bulbs are also grown in water in regular hyacinth glasses. Place a few pebbles and grains of charcoal at the bottom of each glass. The charcoal helps to keep the water pure.

Care
- When the blooming period is over and the leaves turn yellow, bulbs can be stored in a cool, dark place. Bulbs planted in the ground need not be dug up.

Many plants are called hyacinths, but they are members of other genera. Some of these imposters are Grape Hyacinth, Summer Hyacinth and Water Hyacinth.

HYDRANGEA, GARDEN HYDRANGEA
Hydrangea macrophylla

Hanky-Panky in San Francisco

The only time I have been without fresh flowers from the garden
was for a very brief time just after I was married. My husband was
sent to San Francisco and we rented an apartment in an old
Victorian mansion. There was no garden, but the house behind
us had a beautiful one that backed up to our garage. Enormous
hydrangea bushes dripping with lush, pink clusters of flowers
poked their heads above the fence between the two properties.
I resisted for exactly one week, but finally succumbed to the
temptation. From then on we always had a large bowl of luscious,
pink flowers on our coffee table.

It is too bad these glamorous plants can only be grown in mild climates.
They particularly thrive by the seashore. Elsewhere they are house or
hothouse plants, and a favorite potted plant at Easter. Hydrangeas are
small, deciduous shrubs. Most varieties grow 3'-7' high, but some are 12'.

The tiny flowers are in large, ball-shaped clusters and are shades of pink,
red, blue, and white. They bloom in the summer and early fall. Flowers
last a long time, and can change their color like chameleons. If the soil
is too acid, pink flowers turn blue. Add large amounts of lime or superphosphate to an acid soil to keep the flowers pink. Pink and red flowers
can be made to turn blue by adding aluminum sulphate or iron shavings
to the soil. This must be done before buds form.

The clusters of flowers can be sterile or fertile - or both. If all the flowers
are sterile, each tiny bloom is large. Fertile flowers are much smaller.
Plants that have both fertile and sterile flowers are called lace cap
hydrangeas.

HYDRANGEA

Planting
- Young plants are available at nurseries in the spring. Plant in partial shade, under trees, or on a shady side of a house.
- Plant in a rich soil with good drainage, either in the ground or in pots.
- Makes good container plants.

Care
- Feed regularly with a well-balanced fertilizer.
- Keep faded flowers cut.
- Prune in the fall when blooming period is through. Remove all weak stems, and lightly prune the remaining stems. Plants can also be cut back to 10" from the ground. The following year, blooms will be large and plants will remain the same size as they were.
- Softwood cuttings can be made after pruning. See Chapter Fourteen on "How to beat Inflation by Propagation."

Care of Indoor Plants
- Keep well watered, but do not let soil get soggy.
- Do not keep in direct sunlight.
- After blooming, cut plant to about 8" high. Repot in a rich soil. If possible, keep plant outdoors until the frosts arrive. In mild climates, plants can be cut back and planted in the garden.

ICELAND POPPY

Papaver nudicaule

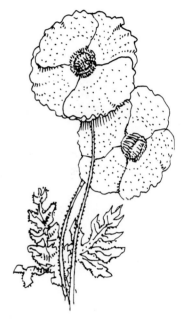

New strains of iceland poppies are constantly being developed. Many people have luck growing them. I wish I knew their secret. The first three years I grew them they were spectacular, but they have been flops recently. I have been lazy about feeding them regularly, and this might be the answer.

Plants are perennials, but in warm climates are treated as annuals. They grow in small, low clumps. Flowers on long 1'-2' stems keep developing week after week, and in mild climates they bloom all winter and spring until hot weather arrives. In cold climates they bloom in the summer and fall. The colors are bright shades of yellow, orange, salmon, rose, cream, and white. Many are variegated. The large Champagne Bubble varieties are quite spectacular.

Planting

- In cold climates, plant young plants in the spring and summer, and in mild climates, in October through December.
- Plant in full sun in a soil that has good drainage.

Care

- Do not overwater. If water accumulates around their roots, plants will die. If plants do not get enough water, buds will fall off.
- Keep flowers picked for more bloom.
- Feed regularly with a well-balanced fertilizer.
- Sear ends of stems when flowers are cut for arrangements.

Iceland poppies are as temperamental as an overrated movie star. Sometimes they bloom and sometimes they don't.

IMPATIENS, PATIENCE, BUSY LIZZIE   *Impatiens wallerana*

Plants are perennials, but are usually grown as annuals in cold climates. There are many varieties which vary in size from 2'-3' high to 4"-8" high. The brilliant colors of the flowers are bright scarlet, pink, salmon, red, purple and white. The hybrid 'Rose Bud' has soft pink double flowers which actually resemble small roses. Many varieties have been brought from New Guinea where they grow wild, and interesting new hybrids are being developed. Some have variegated leaves and can be grown in full sun. Plants grow fast, bloom profusely, and are prolific. They are also splashy in hanging baskets.

Impatiens are as dependable as the rising of the moon and the setting of the sun. They are as sturdy as the Brooklyn Bridge and as magnificent as the Grand Canyon. Impatiens are considered by many to be the most colorful and successful plant for summer bloom in shady spots in the garden.

Planting
- Plant young plants or sow seeds in the early spring in a shady spot in the garden, in pots, window boxes, planters or hanging baskets.
- Plants like a rich, moist soil, but will grow in almost any kind.
- New plants are easily grown from cuttings.

Care
- Keep well-watered or they will wilt before your eyes.
- When plants get leggy, pinch back the long, straggly stems after new leaves begin to grow from bare stems. Plants will probably die if cut back in the winter.
- In mild climates, if plants are left in the ground they reseed themselves profusely.
- If plants are in containers, they should be dug up and thinned out every few years.

IRIS

Clovis and the Purple Iris

In the Fifth Century AD, the Roman Empire finally collapsed
with a low rumble. Alamanni, Burgundians, Goths, Lombards,
Vandals, and the arch villain of them all, Attila the Hun, were
roaming and ravaging Europe. Clovis was king of the Franks, and
was desperately endeavoring to keep all barbarians out of Gaul.

During one of the many battles with the Alamanni, Clovis and
his army were forced to retreat. All went well until they were
abruptly stopped by a very wide river. Clovis had just recently
become a Christian, and he fell to his knees, bowed his head,
and prayed to God. When he looked up, he saw a beautiful,
purple iris growing in the middle of the river. He then knew it
was shallow enough for his army to ford and all were saved. In
gratitude, he made the iris his emblem.

Clovis began to have many victories, and he reunified the
Roman-Gallic territory as the Frankish kingdom. He allied
himself with the Catholic Church and established a small town
called Paris as his capital. Thus began the Merovingian dynasty,
and its emblem, the iris, eventually evolved into the fleur-de-lis.

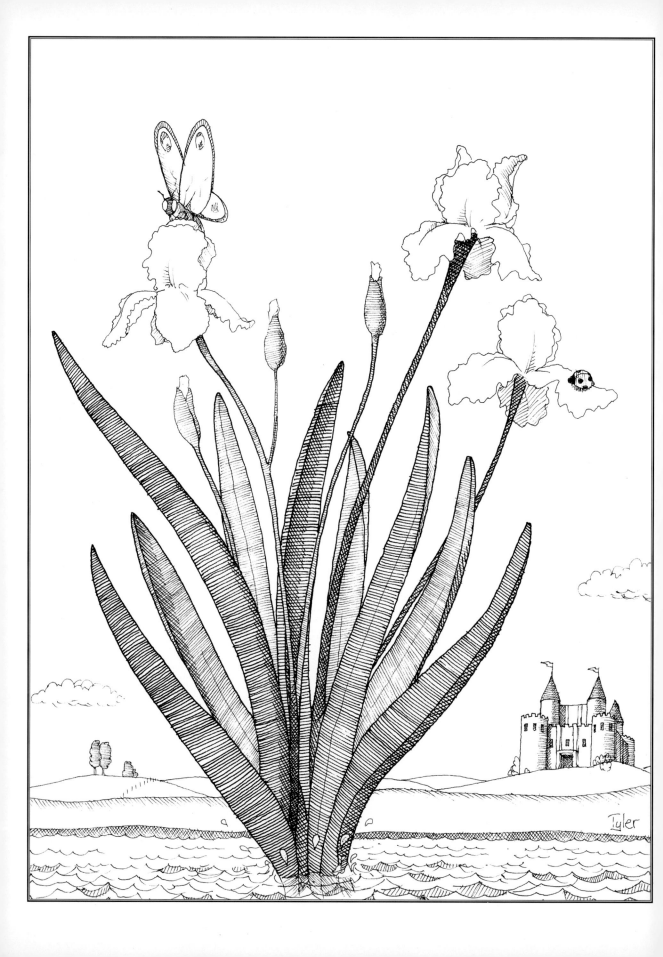

IRIS

Irises are bulbs and rhizomes that thrive in moist sections of the country, but are successfully grown in many other areas. There are over 200 different species and thousands of hybrids. All have leaves that are shaped like swords. Most bloom in the spring and summer.

The many species have been divided into four main groups: Bearded, Beardless, Bulbous, and Crested.

Bearded Irises

These are the best known and most popular of all the irises. There are so many varieties even a nuclear physicist would have a difficult time remembering them. All have one thing in common - a beard or tuft of hair on their falls. The colors and color combinations of the flowers are ad infinitum. They bloom early or late in the spring and vary in height from 10" to 2'-4'. For a selection of magnificent hybrids, write Wayside Gardens, Hodges, South Carolina, 29695, and ask for their catalogue.

Beardless Irises

The irises in this group vary greatly in size and appearance, but all are minus beards on their falls. Some of the species are Japanese Iris (*I. ensata*), Gladwin Iris (*I. foetidissima*), Siberian Iris (*I. sibirica*), Western Blue Flag (*I. missouriensis*), Yellow Flag or Yellow Water Iris (*I. pseudacorus*), Winter Iris (*I. unguicularis*), and Louisiana Irises (Consists of more than three species).

Bulbous Irises

These irises are bulbs that bloom in the spring. They are excellent for cutting and are the irises which are usually sold in floral shops. They are also spectacular in the garden. Spanish Iris (*I. xiphium*), Dutch Iris (Hybrid of Spanish Iris), English Iris (*I. xiphioides*), and Violet-Scented Iris (*I. reticulata*) are all bulbous irises.

"And 'tis my faith,

that every flower enjoys

the air it breathes."

William Wordsworth

IRIS

Crested Irises

There are several species that belong to this category. They are all similar to the bearded irises, but are smaller and have a narrow crest at the base of their falls. A hardy species is *Iris cristata* which creeps along the ground and makes an excellent ground cover as well as a good plant for the rock garden. *Iris japonica* is often called orchid iris because of its beauty.

Planting
- In cold climates plant in the spring in full sun, and in mild climates plant in spring or fall in partial shade. Ask your local nurseryman the best planting time for your area.
- Place rhizomes horizontally 1'-2' apart just below soil level. Plant smaller ones closer. Point the growing end in the direction you want it to spread.
- Most irises like an acid soil and good drainage. If soil is on the alkaline side, make a mixture of 2 gallons water and 1 ounce aluminum sulfate and pour around plants once or twice a year.
- Plant all bulbous irises 4" deep and 4" apart in a light soil with good drainage.

Care
- Water well after planting or transplanting and also when plants are growing and blooming.
- Feed in early spring and once again after blooming period.
- In cold climates, mulch plants in the winter.
- Divide clumps every three or four years in the late summer or fall when they get crowded. Replant healthy rhizomes and throw away the old, woody ones. The leaves and roots can be cut to 3"-6" before transplanting.
- When flowers of bulbous iris die and foliage has yellowed, bulbs can be dug up and stored in a cool, dry place or they can be left in the ground. In cold climates, mulch bulbs if they are left in the ground.

JOHNNY-JUMP-UP
Viola tricolor

Johnny-jump-ups are annuals or short lived perennials. Their stems are delicate and grow 6"-12" high. Flowers are tricolored in different shades of purple, yellow, and a touch of white. Newer varieties have a mixture of yellow, violet, apricot, and red. They are good in borders, mixed with other flowers, in pots or window boxes, and are colorful in hanging baskets. Plants self-sow profusely and literally "jump up" all over the garden and between bricks. After blooming, plants disappear, but pop up again in another spot.

Planting

- In mild climates, plant in fall for spring bloom, and in cold climates, in spring for spring and summer bloom.
- Plant in full sun. Place close together so they can help support each other, or plant near a larger plant they can lean on.
- Not particular about type of soil.

Care

- Feed occasionally with a well-balanced fertilizer.
- Do not let plants dry out. They like to be on the moist side.
- After blooming, cut them back and they will probably bloom again.
- Do not let plants get leggy. Pinch them back when this happens.

Johnny-jump-ups are closely related to and resemble small pansies.

KNIPHOFIA, RED-HOT POKER PLANT *Kniphofia uvaria*

Kniphofias are perennials that grow in large clumps of leaves that resemble fencing swords. Flowers tower above the leaves on long stems and look like "bombs bursting in air". They also look like tiny rockets on their way to Mars, or flamenco dancers about to snap their castanets and stamp their feet.

There are many varieties of Kniphofia. Some are dwarfs with flowers 2' high and others have 3'-6' high blooms. Flowers are a flaming orange-red, yellow, near white, and coral. They bloom in the spring, summer or fall, depending upon the area.

Planting
- Plant in spring in average soil that is well-drained. They do not like a rich soil.
- Plant in a sheltered but sunny spot. Strong winds can damage the heavy flowers on their tall stems.
- Plant 18" apart. They are effective in large borders or with other flowers as accents.

Care
- Keep well watered during growing period.
- Feed occasionally with a well-balanced fertilizer.
- Cut off spikes after they bloom, and when the blooming period is over, cut off the old leaves at the base. Can be propagated by root division.
- In cold climates, either give the plants a good mulch or dig up the rhizomes and store in a cool, dry spot. There are many new hybrids that are hardy and need only be mulched in the winter time.

There is nothing subtle

about this plant - not even

its name - which it got from

a German professor.

LILY, TIGER LILY, EASTER LILY
Lilium

When is a lily a lily? When it has six anthers and is more regal than all the other so-called lilies. Many flowers that belong to entirely different genera have lily as a pseudonym. A few are Lily of the Nile, Lily of the Valley, Calla Lily, Water Lily, Kaffir Lily, and Daylily.

True lilies are bulbs, and there are many species. Some are: madonna lily (*L. candidum*), tiger lily (*L. lancifolium*) and Easter lily (*L. longiflorum*). Many exquisite and sturdy new hybrids and strains have been developed. There are so many hybrids they have been classified into eight main divisions. A few are: Asiatic, American, Candidum, and Oriental.

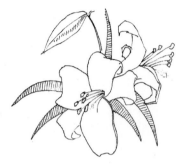

Lilies are easy to grow and require little care. With a proper mulch they can survive most winters. If bulbs are left in the ground, they multiply and readily naturalize. Plants vary in height from 3'-7' high. One bulb will produce between 4 and 15 buds. Flowers have a wide range of colors from pure white to deep red. Many have beautiful shades of yellow, pink, and orange. Some bloom in late May and others in late September, but most bloom during the summer.

"Consider the lilies of the field, how they grow . . . even Solomon in all his glory was not arrayed like one of these."

Bible, Matthew 6:28-29

Planting
- Plant in late fall or early spring as soon as possible after receiving them.
- Plants do best in light or filtered shade.
- Bulbs can be started in wet sand or peat moss.
- Place some bonemeal and sand at the bottom of planting hole and plant in a rich soil that has lots of organic matter such as ground bark, peat moss, or leaf mold.
- Plant 3"-4" deep. Plant small ones less deep, and large ones a little deeper. Place 6"-12" apart in clumps of three or more.

LILY

Care
- Keep moist at all times, but do not let soil get soggy.
- Feed regularly with a well-balanced fertililizer. One well-known grower uses a 5-10-10 formula.
- In hot climates put a 2" mulch of natural leaf mold on plants to keep soil cool and moist.

Things My Mother Never Told Me
- Lily bulbs are never completely dormant and must never be allowed to dry out.
- When stalks of flowers are picked, unopened buds bloom after picking.
- When cutting flowers for arrangements, leave at least 1/3 or more of the stem. Bulbs need nourishment from stems and foliage for next year's growth.

LILY-OF-THE-VALLEY
Convallaria majalis

Plants thrive in cold weather. They are not successfully grown in mild climates, and in hot climates they simply don't survive. They are enchantingly beautiful when naturalized under trees. Plants grow from pips, which are small, upright roots, and they bloom in the spring.

Planting
- Plant pips in September-December in a rich soil with lots of humus.
- Plant in clumps with crowns near soil level. Pips can be planted "pip to pip".

Care
- Every year, preferably in December, put organic fertilizer such as ground bark, leaf mold, or peat moss on top of soil where pips are planted.
- Divide clumps when they get crowded.
- Do not cut leaves when cutting flowers. This will interfere with next year's growth.

Bridal bouquets of lily-of-the-valley are as traditional as wreaths of holly at Christmas.

Growing Lily-of-the-Valley Indoors
- Pre-chilled pips are available at many nurseries in December and January for potting indoors.
- Potting mediums can be sand, sphagnum moss, or peat moss. Use any size pot, and fill entirely with pips.
- Keep well watered, and do not place in direct sunlight.
- In cold areas, after plants bloom, take pips from their pots and plant in the garden. In other areas, remove dirt from pips, put in plastic bags, and keep in the refrigerator until the following year. Then repot them.

LOBELIA

Lobelia erinus

"Am I Blue! Am I Blue!"

Words from an old song

There are many blues. The Blue Grotto, True Blue, St. Louis Blues, The Blue of the Night, Heavenly Blue, The Blue Danube, Picasso's Blue Period, and the magnificent blues of lobelias. These blues are dynamic and vibrant, yet subtle and sophisticated. The Wise Old Owl says all gardens should have a touch of blue, and lobelias provide the classiest shades around. There are also pink, purplish, and white lobelias, but these are not in the same league with the blues. If you have small children or large animals - or large children and small animals - it is a good idea to plant lobelias in pots or other containers as plants are very delicate and can be destroyed by a strong sneeze.

Lobelias are small, dainty annuals that make excellent borders when planted alone or when mixed with other flowers. There are also some trailing varieties that are great in hanging baskets or cascading over a wall.

In mild areas, flowers bloom from late spring to late fall, and plants will survive a mild winter. In cold areas, they bloom from late spring until the first frosts. Plants readily reseed and often appear unannounced in flower beds and between bricks. Three popular varieties are 'Cambridge Blue' (light blue), 'Crystal Palace' (Dark blue) and 'Emperor William' (Medium blue).

Planting
- Young plants are available at nurseries in the spring.
- Plant in partial shade in hot areas, and in full sun in cool and coastal regions.

Care
- Keep plants moist at all times, and feed regularly with a well-balanced fertilizer.
- After blooming, shear off dead flowers and hopefully plants will bloom again.

MARGUERITE, PARIS DAISY
Chrysanthemum frutescens

Marguerites are perennials and the daisylike flowers are yellow, white, or pink. They are single or double and some have cushion centers and others are shaped like buttons. Plants like mild climates and freeze in cold weather.

Planting
- Small bedding plants are available at nurseries in early spring. Larger plants are also sold in 4" or gallon cans.
- Plant 2"-4" apart in full sun in a soil with good drainage. In hot areas, plant in partial shade.

Care
- Plants like lots of water. Do not let soil dry out.
- Feed regularly with a balanced fertilizer.
- Pinch or cut off faded flowers. This is a real chore, but it pays dividends with many more blooms and a well groomed plant.
- Lightly prune occasionally, but do not prune severely because new growth is rarely produced from old wood.
- When plants get straggly, replace with new ones.
- Make cuttings from side shoots in fall or early spring.

Marguerites are many things to many people. Florists sell them in winter and early spring as potted plants. Struggling young career people buy them as cut flowers because the price is right, and landscape architects use them for instant foliage in new gardens as small plants quickly grow into small shrubs.

MARIGOLD

Tagetes erecta &
Tagetes patula

The Disappearing Marigolds

Every summer I plant marigolds in a bed by my front door. A few years ago I bought the entire supply of a spectacular new hybrid from all the local nurseries. I left town a few days, and when I returned, all but one of my new marigold plants had disappeared. I called my Old Gardening Friend with the High Rubber Boots and told him I was coming right over to discuss an urgent matter. "Get out the ice, please," I hastily added.

When I entered his patio, a wondrous, fluffy, mongrel dog named Corky greeted me. The patio was filled with pots of pink and salmon begonias, vividly colored impatiens, hanging baskets of dancing fuchsias - and pots and pots of my hybrid marigolds. I was stunned. "So this is what happened to my new plants!" I muttered to myself as I slowly and dejectedly walked home in utter disbelief.

As I was opening my door, I heard a strange noise in my barren marigold bed. The one remaining plant was slowly disappearing into the earth. Some supernatural force was moving it downward. Suddenly it was gone. I stood transfixed. When I recovered my senses, I realized I had wrongly accused my old gardening friend of being a thief.

I hurriedly ran back to his house, patted Corky on the head, and knocked on the door. My old friend greeted me and asked, "What the hell took you so long?" I never told him. After my first martini - very dry with a twist - I began jabbering about the strange happenings in my marigold bed. My friend just stared at me and bellowed, "You stupid fool! You have a gopher."

MARIGOLD

Marigolds are annuals and are native to Mexico and South America. They were great favorites of the Aztecs and Incas. These easy-to-grow plants have splashy, vivid flowers which bloom all summer. They are single or double, and the colors are orange, yellow, and maroon. Many are bi-colored.

There are two major species, the American or African Marigold (*Tagetes erecta*) and the French Marigold (*Tagetes patula*). Most varieties of American marigolds are tall hybrids (2'-3' high) with double flowers, and others are 12"-20" high. French marigolds are smaller and grow 6"-18" high. There is an Extra Dwarf Double strain 6" high with many flowers, and these plants are good for borders or in pots.

Horticulturists have been on a spree developing new hybrids of marigolds.

Planting
- Marigolds are easy to grow from seeds which can be planted directly in the ground. They germinate in 3-6 days.
- Plant young plants in full sun in the spring after frosts. Plant tall ones 10"-12" apart and deeper than the others. Medium ones 8"-10", and smaller ones 6"-8" apart.
- Not particular about soil, but should have good drainage.

Care
- For bushier plants, pinch them back when they are about 6" high.
- Feed occasionally and keep dead flowers picked. Stake tall plants.
- When it is hot, water daily.
- Carefully cultivate around plants as roots are shallow and can be harmed.

MORNING GLORY

Ipomoea nil &
Ipomoea tricolor

Morning Glories are summer annuals, and are beautiful fast growing vines. They quickly cover trellises, fences, stone walls, and old tree trunks. Occasionally they are used as ground covers.

Flowers open in the morning and fade in the afternoon. They are blue, lavender, red, pink, white, bicolored, striped, and multicolored, and they bloom from June or July until November or the frosts.

Planting
- Many nurseries do not carry young plants, but they are easily started from seeds. These can be sown indoors and transplanted outside later, or they can be planted directly in the ground in March or April. To speed germination, soak seeds in tepid water for a few hours, or cut a small notch in the hard coat with a knife.
- Plant in full sun.
- Plant seeds 1/2" deep and about 6" apart in average soil with good drainage.

Care
- Do not overwater and let soil dry out between waterings when plants are established. If watered too much, large leaves and few flowers will be produced.
- Do not feed.
- Save seeds to be sown the following year. Plants often self-sow.

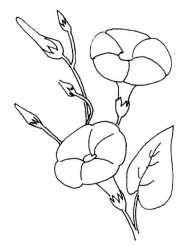

In many parts of the

country, particularly in

cities, morning glories have

become almost as extinct as

triceratops, rumble seats,

and the two-step.

NARCISSUS-DAFFODIL
Narcissus

Daffodil is the common name for all members of the narcissus genus. Many people call the large trumpet varieties daffodils, and the smaller cupped ones narcissus. Others mistakenly refer to narcissus and daffodils as jonquils, which is a division of narcissus.

All narcissus are bulbs that bloom early in spring. They are hardy and can be grown in all climates. If left in the ground, they multiply year after year. Gophers hate the bulbs because they are poisonous if eaten. Plants are spectacular when naturalized in lawns or woody areas. Hardy varieties such as trumpet and large-cupped daffodils do exceptionally well in the Northwestern and Northeastern parts of the country as well as in Michigan near the lake. Flowers are different shades of yellow, orange, white, and some are near-pink. Many are bicolored and some have small touches of red. The smaller flowers are usually very fragrant.

"Daffodils that come before

the swallow dares, and take

the winds of March

with beauty."

Shakespeare

Planting
- Buy No. 1 double nose bulbs. These have two points on top and will produce two stalks instead of one.
- Plant as early in fall as possible. In warm climates plant in November when the soil cools.
- Plant in a soil with good drainage and plant in sun or partial shade. Must be in partial shade in hot climates.
- Plant large bulbs about 6" deep and 8" apart. Plant smaller bulbs closer together and less deep. Place a handful of sand under each bulb.

Care
- Give soil a good soaking after planting, and keep well-watered.
- Plants do not need to be fed the first year.
- After blooming, let foliage dry out before removing.
- Divide bulbs every three or four years after foliage has died. If possible, replant them at once.

NASTURTIUM

Tropaeolum majus

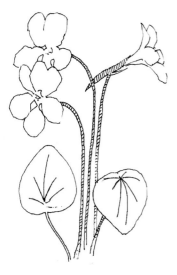

The Broken Tiffany Lamp

When I was small, we had a bed of nasturtiums by the back door of our house. Today, whenever I see these flowers, I think of that house and my dog Peege, who was a wire-haired fox terrier. He loved to chew things. In the summer, my father kept his straw hat on a table next to a beautiful Tiffany lamp. One day when we returned from a spin in our new Pierce Arrow, we found Peege blissfully sitting on the table chewing the hat. The Tiffany lamp lay in pieces on the floor, but the nasturtiums were still blooming by the back door to help cheer us up.

Nasturtiums are cheerful and happy flowers. They are perennials but are usually treated as annuals. Plants are fast growing and require very little care, and they readily reseed themselves. Some varieties climb and others trail on the ground. There are also compact, dwarf plants that grow about a foot high. Flowers are single or double and are in bright colors of yellow, orange, many shades of red, and a creamy white. In mild climates they bloom almost year round, and in cold areas they bloom in spring until the frosts. In hot climates they bloom in the winter until the summer heat arrives.

Planting

- Young plants are often available at nurseries in spring, but nasturtiums are easy to grow from seed. In mild climates, sow seeds in fall or spring, and in cold areas in early spring.
- Plant seeds in full sun about 4" apart. Thin them if necessary once they are up. Seeds take about ten days to germinate.
- Plants prefer sandy soil with good drainage but will grow in almost any kind.

NASTURTIUM

Care
- If plants are in a good soil, they do not need to be fed.
- Keep plants on the dry side except when it is hot.
- Watch for snails, slugs and aphids.

Things My Mother Never Told Me
- The flowers, leaves, and seed pods of nasturtiums are good when eaten. They are high in vitamin C, and have a peppery taste that adds a zing to many recipes.
- Tender leaves are often used in salads.
- Seed pods can be pickled and used as a substitute for capers. Pick pods when they are small and green. Soak them in salted water for three days. Change water each day. Dry pods and put in a jar with some minced onion and chopped tarragon.
Boil 2 cups white vinegar, salt and pepper to taste, and a dash of cayenne for ten minutes and pour over seed pods.
Put a tight lid on the jar and refrigerate at least one week before using.

NICOTIANA OR FLOWERING TOBACCO *Nicotiana alata*

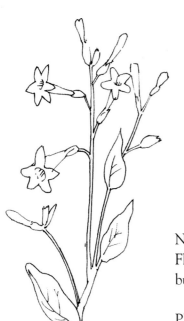

Gramps and the Hooker

An old man with a cane walked slowly down a crowded street. He came to a bench, paused briefly, and sank down to rest. A young girl with a beehive hairdo, high boots, and a sweater that was at least three sizes too small, walked up with hips swinging. She whispered a few words to him, and he told her to get lost. As she stomped away she yelled back and said, "What are you saving yourself for, Gramps, the Senior Prom!" If you have never grown nicotiana, what are you saving yourself for?

Nicotiana is a fragrant perennial that is usually treated as an annual. Flowers of many varieties only open in the evenings or on cloudy days, but new strains have been developed that open in the daytime.

Plants grow 2'-3' high, and some varieties grow 1' high. Stems and leaves are slightly sticky. The dainty flowers resemble tiny stars and are white, greenish yellow, and lime. They bloom in summer until the frosts. The Sensation strain has red, rose, coral, and chocolate flowers. Many varieties readily reseed themselves.

Planting
- In the spring, plant young plants 10" apart in full sun or partial shade. Also effective when massed in groups in a flower bed.
- Not particular about soil. If area is windy or damp, plant in a warm, sheltered spot.

Care
- Needs little care.
- Feed occasionally with a well-balanced fertilizer.

ORIENTAL POPPY

Papaver orientale

Oriental poppies are flamboyant perennials that love cold climates and do not do well in areas where winters are warm. The sturdy, temperamental plants grow 2'-4' high and are dormant in midsummer. The single or double flowers are 6" wide, and are flaming shades of red and orange. There are also more subdued colors of white, rose, and lavender. Flowers have a texture of crinkled silk and bloom in early spring.

Planting

- Plant in August or September in full sun in a rich, loamy soil with good drainage.
- Plant at least 1 1/2'-2' apart with crowns 2" below soil level.

Care

- Do not overwater as plants hate soggy roots.
- Stake plants before they become top-heavy.
- Plants will bloom very little the first season.
- Do not let seed pods develop. Remove them if they do.
- Cut back foliage after it has died.
- Cut flowers for bouquets before buds open and sear ends of stems to make flowers last longer.

Ah so, Confucius say,

"This is one big poppy!"

PANSY

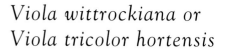

Viola wittrockiana or
Viola tricolor hortensis

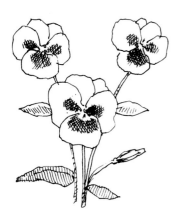

Pansies are perennials but are usually treated as annuals, and they grow 6"-8" high. They are used in borders, as ground covers, in pots and hanging baskets. Flowers have a multitude of colors in many shades of purple, deep red, white, yellow, blue, apricot, pink, and many are bicolored. The Swiss Giants and the Majestic Giant strains have large flowers 2"-4" across. Some have dark faces of a contrasting color and others are without faces. In mild climates they bloom in winter and spring until midsummer. In cold climates they bloom in spring and summer.

Planting
- In mild climates, plant young plants in fall or early spring. In cold climates, plant in early spring after frosts.
- In coastal areas pansies can be planted in full sun, but they prefer partial shade in others. In hot climates, they must be in full shade.
- Plant 6"-8" apart in a rich soil with good drainage.

Care
- Never let plants dry out as they like a moist soil.
- Pinch back small plants to make them bushy, and pinch back again if they get leggy.
- Feed with a complete fertilizer or fish emulsion every two weeks.
- Keep dead flowers picked for longer blooming period.
- Do not pile dirt around plants as this could cause a fungus which will rot entire plants. This disease often strikes, particularly if pansies were in the same place the previous year. Spray with a fungicide.
- Dig up plants when they stop blooming or get too ragged. This usually happens by the middle of summer and earlier in hot areas.

The pansy is one of the oldest flowers to be cultivated, and it is also one of the most popular. In 1835 there were 400 varieties, and today there are over 4,000.

PANSY

Things My Mother Never Told Me

- A simple home remedy for improving the color of pansies is to give them a solution of water and ashes from the fireplace. This is commonly called soot water.
- Culpepper, in his book on herbs, says a strong syrup made by boiling stems and flowers of pansy plants, is an excellent cure for venereal diseases!

". . . and there are pansies,

that's for thoughts."

Shakespeare

PELARGONIUM, GERANIUM

Pelargonium is the name of the genus, and geranium is the common name for most of the species. The three most popular ones are Lady Washington Pelargonium, Common or Garden Geranium, and Ivy Geranium. All are perennials, but in colder climates, they are treated as summer annuals or house plants. All three have the same planting and care so are discussed in one chapter. There are many different varieties in each species.

An old copper bowl

filled with bright red

geraniums is just as

beautiful as a silver vase

filled with roses.

Lady Washington Pelargonium, Martha Washington Geranium
Pelargonium domesticum
This is the most sophisticated species and the one commonly called pelargonium. Individual flowers are larger than those in the other species, and they are in looser clusters. There are many color combinations, and most of them are in subtle shades of pinks and lavenders with dark markings. Plants grow about 3' high and tend to become straggly if not pinched back. Flowers bloom in spring and summer.

Common Geranium, Garden Geranium
Pelargonium hortorum
These geraniums were status symbols during the Victorian era, but when everyone began to cultivate them, they became plebeians in informal gardens. A house in the country is seldom without geraniums climbing over old stone walls or white picket fences. Flowers bloom profusely from spring to late fall and are single or double. There are many shades of pink, red, orange, or white. Plants grow 3' and some are taller.

PELARGONIUM, GERANIUM

Ivy Geranium
Pelargonium peltatum
This is a trailing plant that is excellent in hanging baskets or as a ground cover. Flowers are single or double and are white, lavender, various shades of red, and many are variegated. The most popular color is a soft pink. Visitors to Southern California are always stupified at the vast number of "lawns" that are solid masses of geraniums. Little do they know that thousands of snails and slugs are lurking beneath the leaves. In mild climates flowers bloom almost year round.

Planting for all species
- Young plants are available at local nurseries, but it is much more fun and a lot cheaper to get cuttings from friends or neighbors. Cuttings are easy to grow and don't have to be started in a special rooting soil. Put them in pots with regular potting soil or directly in the ground. The best cuttings are from tender new shoots that appear in spring.
- Plant in full sun. In hot areas, plant in partial shade.
- Plants will grow in average soil with good drainage.

A rose is a rose is a rose, but a pelargonium is also a geranium.

Care for all species
- Do not overwater. Allow soil to dry out before each watering. Plants like to be deep watered.
- Do not overfeed. If plants get too much nitrogen, leaves will be lush, but they will not bloom as much.
- Pinch back young plants to make them bushy, and pinch back again if they get leggy.
- In mild climates, drastically prune back plants in early spring after the frosts.
- Tobacco bud worms often eat holes in buds before they bloom. Spray with Sevin before these pests appear.

PENSTEMON, BEARD TONGUE, BORDER OR GARDEN PENSTEMON

Penstemon gloxinioides

The name penstemon is

derived from the Greek

word for five, which is

"penta". Flowers of this

genus usually have five

stamens. This information

is about as important to

remember as the dates of

the Second Punic War

(218-208 BC).

There are many species of penstemon which grow wild in the Western states. This penstemon is a hybrid of several species. Plants are short-lived perennials but are treated as annuals in cold climates. They grow 2'-4' high and are excellent massed in beds or planted in borders along fences or driveways. Hummingbirds love the nectar from the flowers.

The small tubular flowers are on long spikes and are similar to Canterbury Bells. They are white, scarlet, pink, violet, and rose. In mild climates they bloom in spring and summer. In cold areas they bloom in summer.

Planting
- In cold climates, plant young plants in spring after frosts. In mild ones, plant in spring or fall. If planted in fall, flowers will bloom in April.
- Plant in full sun about one foot apart. In hot climates, plant in partial shade.
- Must have a sandy, well-drained soil to thrive as they are subject to root rot.

Care
- Feed regularly with a well-balanced fertilizer, and stake plants if needed.
- In mild climates, cut plants back one half their height in fall after they have bloomed. Plants can also be divided at this time.
- Softwood cuttings can be made from new growth that appears after plants have been cut back.
- Plants usually need to be replaced every three or four years.

PEONY, HERBACEOUS PEONY
Paeonia

Rain? What Rain?

Once I spent several winter months in the Pacific Northwest. It rained so much all I could relate to was Sadie Thompson. After endless weeks, the deluge finally stopped. The sun shone like a nugget of gold, and the snow-covered peaks of the Cascades sparkled in the glorious sunshine. Puget Sound was the color of dazzling sapphires. Birds filled the forests with a cacophony of sounds, and new leaves on the trees and ferns slowly uncurled. Butterflies burst from their cocoons and rabbits jumped from their warrens. Hundreds of sumptuous peonies, looking like Southern belles dressed in voluminous hoop skirts, burst into bloom. The past dreary, wet days were soon forgotten. Rain? What rain?

Peonies thrive in Northern parts of the United States where winters are long and cold. They are hardy, perennial plants with tuberous roots. They love long, cold winters and hate hot, dry springs, but hot summers do not bother them. The bushy plants grow 2 1/2'-4' high. Established plants in pots and bare-root ones can be bought at nurseries or ordered by catalogue from one of the many growers. There are over 5,000 different varieties from which to choose.

Peonies have magnificent, large flowers with silky petals, and many have a fragrance somewhat like a rose. They are single, semi-double, double, and Japanese type (single flowers with masses of yellow petaloids, which are stamens that have turned into petals). Colors are white, many shades of creams and pinks, salmon, coral, red, and yellow. Blooming period is from mid to late spring, and there are early and late blooming varieties. Flowers are long lasting and if cut at just the right stage, buds can be refrigerated for weeks and brought out to bloom.

PEONY

Planting
- Plant in early fall.
- In cold climates, plant in full sun, and in warmer climates plant in partial shade.
- Carefully select a spot for planting as peonies do not like to be moved and may not bloom the first year after transplanting.
- In cold climates, plant eyes of tubers 2" below the soil. If they are planted deeper, they might not bloom. In warmer climates plant 1 1/2" deep or just below the soil.
- Not too particular about soil, but plants will be healthier and flowers larger if humus is added.
- Plant at least 3' apart in groups of three or more, or plant in large masses. They make good background plants.

Care
- When plants are established, feed with a complete fertilizer. Feed again in spring and once again after plants have bloomed.
- Flowers are heavy and plants need support.
- For large blooms, disbud small side buds and leave one bud at tip of each stem. For smaller and more flowers, do not disbud. Remove faded flowers so they do not form pods.
- In fall when leaves turn brown, cut off stems just barely below surface of soil.
- When clumps get crowded, which might not be for ten or twelve years, divide in fall. Cut off foliage and divide into sections with three or more growth buds, being careful not to injure the tender, pink buds or eyes.
- If flower buds turn brown and leaves become spotted, plants probably have botrytis. This usually occurs during the wet season. Spray with benomyl before buds open, and remove all diseased buds and leaves.

PERIWINKLE, VINCA

Catharanthus roseus
& Vinca rosea

In the East it is called periwinkle, and in the West, vinca - a regional prerogative. Plants are perennials but are usually treated as annuals. There are bushy varieties 1'-2' high and dwarf ones 10" high. They are often planted with zinnias, asters, dahlias, and marigolds. Flowers bloom all summer and into the late fall in mild areas. They are all white, white with a red dot in the center, rosy pink, and light pink. Plants readily self-sow.

Planting
- Young plants are available in flats at nurseries in spring.
- Plant in full sun or partial shade. Plant larger plants about 12" apart and smaller ones closer together.
- Not particular about soil.
- Easy to grow from seed.

Care
- Do not overwater. Plants can withstand a short drought.
- Feed regularly with a well-balanced fertilizer.
- In mild climates, plants can be left in the ground. If they start to look straggly, trim them back. Most gardeners dig up old plants and buy new ones the following spring. I planted some last summer and left them in all winter and they are bushier, healthier and have more flowers this year than last year. Also many seedlings sprang up in bare spots. I do live in a mild climate.

This happy-go-lucky flower

loves hot weather and

would rather be in Phoenix

than in Vermont.

PETUNIA

The Saga of Princess Prunella

Once upon a time a beautiful princess named Prunella lived in the Land of Iz. She was not an ordinary princess who dwelt in a palace. She was a captivating, double ruffled, grandiflora petunia, and she lived in a greenhouse with her sisters. Numerous attendants diligently watered her, fertilized her, and sprayed her with insecticides. Prunella grew into a dazzling beauty.

One day a lady, who wore a battered, straw hat, came to the greenhouse and took Prunella and her sisters to her garden and carefully planted them in a sandy soil with very good drainage. They had the best of care.

Several months later, five large, very black crows flapped their way to a tall eucalyptus tree outside the garden gate. The largest crow flew up to Prunella and said to her, "The great Hades of the Nether World has sent me to bring you back as his 393rd concubine."

Prunella was stunned. She replied, "I refuse to leave this lovely garden and all my sisters." She thought of Daphne, the nymph who turned herself into a laurel tree when Apollo tried to seduce her. Prunella and her sisters decided to swallow some poisonous bug juice, and just before they died they put a curse on the garden. From that day on, no petunias have been able to grow in this garden.

If you have a better explanation of why I can't grow petunias, please let me know.

PETUNIA

Petunia hybrida

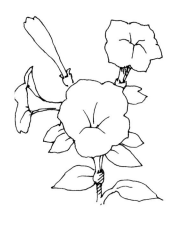

Petunias are perennials but are usually treated as annuals. They are supposedly easy to grow, and I have seen them thriving in many gardens, but I have rotten luck with them. Perhaps my garden is too shady for them.

There are two main varieties of hybrid petunias - Grandiflora and Multiflora. The grandiflora varieties have large flowers and the sturdy plants grow 12"-24" high. Some cascade and are good for hanging baskets and window boxes. The multiflora varieties are about the same height, but plants are more compact and flowers are smaller and more profuse. They are good for mass planting. These new hybrids are sturdy and are fairly resistant to diseases.

Flowers are both single and double. Some are ruffled, fringed, and stripped. Colors are many shades of red and purple, pale yellow, blue, salmon, cream, and white. In mild climates they bloom almost the year round, and elsewhere in late spring and summer until the frosts.

Planting
- In mild climates, plant in fall or spring, and in cold climates in spring after the frosts. Depending upon the variety, plant from 8"-16" apart.
- Petunias like lots of sun and they love hot weather. They prefer a sandy soil with good drainage, but will grow in most kinds.

Care
- When young plants are well established, pinch back about half the plant to make them bushy.
- Feed regularly with a well-balanced fertilizer.
- Pinch back again at the end of summer or when plants get leggy. This will force new growth.

PHLOX, SUMMER PHLOX
Phlox paniculata

Phlox is a longtime favorite in gardens, and many consider it to be the backbone of their garden. Plants thrive in the Eastern and Northwestern parts of the country, but can be grown in many other areas. There is an annual phlox, *P. drummondii,* which is a native of Texas, and it thrives in hot climates and blooms in the summer. Two other species make good ground covers. They are the Trailing Phlox, *P. nivalis,* and Moss Pink, *P. subulata.*

The Summer Phlox is a perennial and grows 3'-5' high. Beautiful new hybrids are constantly being developed. Flowers grow in large clusters on 3'-5' high stems, and colors are many shades of red, purple, and white. Some are variegated. They bloom in summer until the frosts.

Try it. You'll like it!

Planting
- In mild climates, plant in fall or spring. In cold climates, in spring.
- Plant in full sun. They are sun worshippers.
- Not too particular about soil, but will do better in soil that has been well prepared. Plant large varieties 2' apart and smaller ones closer together.

Care
- Keep plants well watered and feed regularly with a well-balanced fertilizer.
- In dry, hot climates, mulch plants in summer. In cold climates, mulch plants in winter.
- Keep faded flowers picked, and in the fall after the blooming season, cut plants to the ground.
- Divide plants every three or four years or when they get crowded. Discard the old, inner sections and replant the strong, young shoots on the outside of clumps.
- Seedlings revert to their original lavender shade.

POINSETTIA

Euphorbia pulcherrima

These dramatic, perennial plants grow outdoors in mild climates, and are indoor plants elsewhere. Outdoor plants grow up to 10'. The so-called flowers are bracts, or modified leaves. They are single and double in flaming red, creamy white, and a beautiful pink, and they often last for two or three months. Variegated varieties have been developed.

Planting

- Plants are available at nurseries, or they can be started from stem cuttings in spring or late summer. Make cuttings 6"-8" long and plant 4" deep in moist sand or other rooting soil.
- Plant in full sun against a wall or fence.
- Plant in a soil with good drainage and one that is slightly acid.

Care

- Plants are sturdy and need little care.
- Cut plants back in spring leaving at least three buds on each stalk. Prune less severely again in summer.
- When new growth appears, feed regularly with a fertilizer high in nitrogen. This helps produce large bracts and improves their color.

POINSETTIA

Care of Poinsettia House Plants

- Immediately remove any tinfoil or other wrapping from pots so plants will get good drainage.
- Keep out of drafts and avoid sudden temperature changes. If possible keep in a sunny spot and keep soil moist but not soggy.
- When plants stop blooming, leaves will begin to drop. Start withdrawing water, and when all leaves have fallen, cut plants back to two buds. Store in a cool, dark spot and water sparingly while plants are dormant. In mild climates, poinsettias can be transplanted in the garden.
- When warm weather arrives, place pots in a sunny spot outdoors and keep them well watered all summer. Feed once a month and prune in July for bushier plants.
- Bring indoors again before weather turns cold, and keep in a dark room at night during the months of October and November. Plants must have 14 hours of darkness while they are setting their buds.

'Tis the season. Ho, Ho, Ho! Fa, la, la, and Bah Humbug. A Christmas without poinsettias is like an ocean without fish and the sky without stars. They are as much a part of the yuletide season as holly, fir trees, Santa Claus, and egg nogs.

PRIMROSE, ENGLISH PRIMROSE
Primula polyantha
& Primula vulgaris

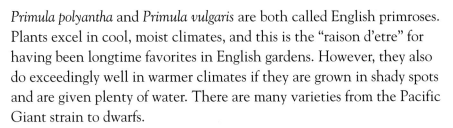

Primula polyantha and *Primula vulgaris* are both called English primroses. Plants excel in cool, moist climates, and this is the "raison d'etre" for having been longtime favorites in English gardens. However, they also do exceedingly well in warmer climates if they are grown in shady spots and are given plenty of water. There are many varieties from the Pacific Giant strain to dwarfs.

Primroses are perennials, but in many climates are often treated as annuals. They make good borders, and are very effective naturalized under trees. They can also be massed in groups for a splash of color or planted in containers.

Flowers are long-lasting. They grow on 8"-12" stems and are strong blues, yellows, reds, and also violet, pink, rust, apricot, and white. In colder climates flowers bloom in April until early June, and in warmer climates from late winter until summer.

Come down the "primrose

path of dalliance" with me.

The words in quotes

are Shakespeare's.

Planting
- In warm climates, plant young plants in late fall. In cold climates, plant in spring after the frosts.
- Plant in a loamy soil with good drainage. Add lots of peat moss or leaf mold to soil before planting.
- Plant young plants 6"-8" apart in partial shade.

Care
- Constantly watch for snails and slugs. Use an entire package of snail bait if necessary.
- Keep plants moist at all times.
- Feed regularly with a fish emulsion or a fertilizer low in nitrogen. Do not feed when plants are dormant.
- In cold climates, mulch plants in winter, and in warm climates, mulch them in summer to keep their roots cool.
- Divide plants every few years when they get crowded. Do this after their blooming period.

PRIMULA, PRIMROSE

Primula malacoides &
Primula obconica

Primula malacoides and *Primula obconicas* are not true twins, but they are of the same genus and are often planted together. The planting and care is the same for both. The *malacoides* are the more delicate of the two. They are often called Fairy Primroses, and the small, dainty flowers are in many lacy whorls along tall slender stems. The flowers of the *obconicas* grow in large, round clusters, and in mild regions they bloom many months of the year. The flowers on both species are in pastel colors of pinks and lavenders, white, and various shades of red. Both are excellent houseplants.

These primulas are perennials, but are usually treated as annuals. They love moist, cool air, and droop in hot weather.

Planting
- In mild climates, plant young plants in the fall. In cold climates, plant in the spring after the frosts.
- Plant in full or partial shade. They will wilt in full sun.
- Easy to grow from seeds. Sow seeds in February or March.
- Plant in a rich soil. Add lots of humus or compost if the soil is poor.

Castor and Pollux

and Romulus and Remus

Care
- Keep plants well watered.
- Feed regularly with a well-balanced fertilizer or fish emulsion.

of the garden.

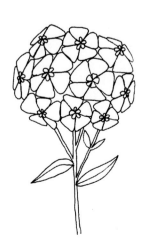

RANUNCULUS, PERSIAN RANUNCULUS, TURBAN RANUNCULUS

Ranunculus asiaticus

A Tribute to a Wonderful Lady

Everyone calls her Auntie Fran. She is a widow who is hovering around eighty. A pacemaker is in her heart, and her hands are crippled with arthritis. Under these circumstances, most people would retire to a rocking chair and fizzle out just like an open bottle of soda pop. Not Auntie Fran. She became the "Vegetable Queen of Oceanside".

After her husband's death, Auntie Fran became very lonely. This is when she decided to become a greengrocer. She painted a sign that said, "Fresh Vegetables for Sale", and her garage was turned into a store. She was still able to drive, and every morning she would go into the back country and fill her station wagon with fresh vegetables, which she bought from local farmers. Her prices were way below those at nearby supermarkets, and her produce was infinitely better.

Many people got to know and love Auntie Fran because of her vegetables. Every Christmas the walls of her house are filled with Christmas cards from her many customers - now her dear friends.

I have a special reason for loving Auntie Fran. She is primarily responsible for my great interest in gardening. Many times when I bought vegetables, I would bring her flowers from my garden. I did not grow them. I had a gardener. One day she gave me 500 ranunculus bulbs, and I decided to plant them myself. When they sprouted and the magnificent, ruffly, double flowers bloomed, I became an instant gardener and have been one ever since.

Last year, the doctors told Auntie Fran she must close her vegetable store as her heart could not stand the strain. She has not retired to a rocking chair, but she has retired to a large, wicker "throne" under the old fig tree where her many friends stop by to chat with her and to sip wine.

RANUNCULUS

Ranunculus are tubers and the beautiful flowers add class and sophistication to a garden. Plants thrive in mild, cool, moist climates. They grow in low clumps with lacy leaves. Flowers are on slender stems 18"-24" high. There are many strains and varieties.

Flowers are semi-double and double, and are different shades of pink, crimson, scarlet, red, orange, yellow, purple, orange-pink, and white. They bloom from spring to early summer.

Planting

- In warm climates, plant anytime after soil is cool between October and January. In cold climates, plant in early spring, or start tubers indoors in moist sand, and plant outside after the frosts. Planting can be staggered for continuous blooms over a long period.
- In hot climates, soak tubers 3-4 hours before planting. Do not do this in other climates.
- Plant in full sun. In hot climates, in partial shade. Soil must have good drainage as tubers are susceptible to root rot.
- Plant tubers 1"-2" deep and about 7" apart with the claws down.

Care

- Water well just after planting as roots will not form until enough moisture has been absorbed to make tubers plump. Do not water again until shoots appear.
- Feed with a balanced fertilizer.
- When flowers are through blooming and the leaves have turned yellow, dig up tubers. Dry them for a few days before storing in a well ventilated, dark place.
- In mild climates, tubers are often left in the ground. Sometimes they come up and sometimes they don't.

RHODODENDRON

Rhododendrons are beautiful evergreen or deciduous shrubs that thrive in areas where there is much rain. They are native to many parts of the country. The Blue Ridge Mountains are aflame in spring with magnificent wild species, and the Pacific Northwest is famous for its "rhodies". There are thousands of named varieties and about 800 species, which are divided into series and sub-series. Consult your nurseryman or local arboretum as to which ones are best for your area.

Some rhododendrons are 50' high (in Asia) and others are only a few inches high. There are multitudes of various sizes in between. The splashiest plants are the large, flowering hybrids. Magnificent flowers grow in round clusters. Colors are many shades of red from a soft pink to a scarlet, orange from a delicate apricot to a strong salmon, various purples, and white. Blooming season differs with the area and species, but it is anywhere from February to late May.

Planting
- Plants in tubs are available at nurseries in spring. Many are in full bloom. In mild climates, they can also be planted in fall.
- Plant in filtered shade. They do well under tall trees. In areas where summers are cool, can be in full sun.
- Plant in a rich, acid soil. Add leaf mold or peat moss, and ground bark to soil before planting.
- Place top of root ball just above level of soil. The fibrous roots need lots of oxygen.

When rhododendrons are in full bloom, they are as spectacular as the Triumphal March in Verdi's "Aida" and as ostentatious as the finale in the Folies-Bergères.

RHODODENDRON

Care of Rhododendrons
- Pinch back tips of young plants to make them bushy.
- Feed once a month with an acid fertilizer when new growth begins in spring. Stop feeding in August.
- Keep faded flowers picked, and keep soil moist but never allow it to get soggy as this could cause root rot.
- During hot spells, water daily in the morning or late afternoon.
- Never use a hoe or other tool near a plant. Roots are close to the surface and could be injured. Put a mulch of redwood shavings around plants.
- Drastic pruning on older plants that need shaping should be done in early spring. The best time for a light pruning is when plants are blooming.

Things My Mother Never Told Me
- Rhododendron leaves are poisonous if eaten.
- Plants are often damaged if there is a quick change of temperature.

ROSE (Her Serene Highness)
Rosa

"My Luv is Like a Red, Red Rose"

Throughout the centuries, poets, philosophers, painters, and songwriters have praised the beauty of the rose. In 600 BC Sappho, the Greek poetess, wrote an "Ode to the Rose" and called it the "queen of flowers". Many years later, Robert Burns wrote, "O, my luv is like a red, red rose", and everyone with the possible exception of the aborigines in New Guinea has heard what Gertrude Stein said about the rose.

Nothing, not even a priceless Sèvres vase or a Ming Dynasty horse, can do more for a room than a large bowl of roses in full bloom. Bring your favorite person breakfast in bed and put a red rose in a silver vase on the tray. You might have to cancel all your appointments for the rest of the day.

"Gather ye rosebuds

while ye may."

Robert Herrick

Roses are classified according to their structure and growth. Many roses quiver on the borderlines of the following classifications:

Old-Fashioned Roses are the grandparents of all roses. Tea and China roses are in this classification.

Polyanthas are compact bushes with large clusters of small flowers.

Hybrid Teas have large blooms and are by far the most popular.

Floribundas are the result of crossing polyanthas with hybrid teas for better formed plants and larger flowers in each cluster.

Grandifloras have large flowers in small clusters and are defined by British rosarians as "Floribundas, hybrid tea type".

Also Climbing Roses, Tree or Standard Roses, and Miniature Roses

ROSE

How to Select a Rose

- Write to the American Rose Society, P.O. Box 30,000, Shreveport, Louisiana 71130, and ask for their "Handbook for Selecting Roses".
- Send for a catalogue of one of the nurseries that specialize in roses.
- Select an All-American winner. Each year the American Rose Society names a new rose the All-American Winner for that year. If AARS (All-American Rose Selection) 1992, is on a rose label, it means that rose was the All-American for 1992.
- Visit a rose garden when it is in full bloom. Almost every community has at least one public rose garden. Even Virginia City, Nevada, the lively old mining town on the Comstock Lode, has one next to the jailhouse.

"I see and know not why

Thorns live and roses die."

Walter Savage Landor

Buying Rose Plants

- Most plants sold are bare-root, and these are the best buys. The American Association of Nurserymen has standards for the quality of plants, and each plant is classified as No. 1, No. 1 1/2, and No. 2.
- When buying a bare-root plant, be sure the eyes on the canes are plump and ready to grow, but not yet growing. Inspect roots for any possible damage.

Planting

- Can be planted any time during their dormant season when soil is not frozen. In mild climates, roses are usually planted in January or February. Plant bare roots as soon as possible after receiving them.
- Plant in full sun at least 3' apart. Roses must have good air circulation.
- Plant in a soil with good drainage.
- See page 151 for further planting information.

ROSE

Care

- After their dormant season, feed regularly with a complete fertilizer or a special rose food.
- Roses need lots of water. Deep water them once a week, and more often if it is hot. Do not water overhead as this could cause mildew.
- If weather is hot, mulch plants with an organic mulch, but do not use peat moss as it quickly dries out.
- Remove all buds except one on each stem for large flowers.
- Cut roses in the morning when the dew is still on the petals. Cut just above a set of five leaflet leaves.
- Aphids and mildew are two of the many bugs and diseases that attack roses. Cutworms also bury themselves among bud petals. There are sprays formulated just for roses to combat these pests.
- Once a year give plants a major pruning. In mild climates prune in January or February, and in colder climates, in March or April. Cut back canes 1/2 to 1/3 the length of growth that was new the past year. In mild climates, leave at least 18". In cold climates, bushes can be cut back shorter. Also cut out all dead and straggly branches and any that cross each other.
- In cold winters protect plants by making mounds of soil about a foot high around them. Tie canes together. When mounds have frozen, cover them with branches or some other light material. This will keep plants at an even temperature. Remove mounds as soon as frosts are over.

ROSE

Planting Roses Whilst Drinking Martinis

- Make a pitcher of 4 jiggers of gin to 1/2 jigger of vermouth. Add ice cubes and stir 96 times. Fill a long-stemmed glass with the nectar and add a twist of lemon. Take a few sips, and then take the pitcher of martinis and glass to the garden.
- Dig a hole large enough to hold all extended roots of rose bush. 18" wide and 18" deep is the average size. Take a few more sips before proceeding.
- Mix soil from the hole with 1/3 humus or peat moss. Put 1 cup bonemeal or superphosphate in bottom of hole, and cover this with a small mound of the mixed soil. Take a few more sips.
- Place rose bush on top of mound. Spread roots and tuck soil under them so there are no air pockets. Fill hole 3/4 full with the mixed soil and gently firm dirt with your feet or a spade. Water and let soil settle. This will give you time to finish your martini and pour another one.
- Fill hole with remaining soil. In warm climates, the knob or bud union on the plant should be slightly above ground level, and in cold climates, it should be slightly below ground level. Thoroughly water again and take a few more sips.
- If the weather is cold and windy - or warm and dry - make a mound 6"-8" high around the cane, but remember to remove it when leaves appear.
- Finish pitcher of martinis and take a long nap.

SALVIA, SCARLET SAGE
Salvia splendens

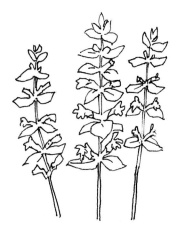

A Peruvian Happening

The first time I saw scarlet sage, or salvia, was in a garden near Lima, Peru. The blooms were fiery red and were startlingly dramatic against the bleak, barren foothills of the Andes. I expressed my admiration for this striking plant, and my gracious host gave me a few seed pods to take back to the States. I thanked him, put the pods in my purse, and promptly forgot about them until months later after I had returned home.

At this point in my life I didn't know an epidendrum from an epiphyllum and terms like mulch, mealybug, and Malathion simply were not in my vocabulary. However, I bravely proceeded to plant my seeds in an old, discarded nursery flat I found in the garage.

Several weeks later, my husband casually asked me if I had noticed all the funny looking shoots in an old flat near the rusty spades and shovels. I was dumbfounded. My seeds had survived a trip across the equator into a strange hemisphere and were actually sprouting in dirt that was of such poor quality even weeds refused to grow in it. A veritable miracle had happened, and ever since that day my husband calls me Luther Burbank.

SALVIA

There are many species of salvia, but the most spectacular and popular annual is the blazing red one called Scarlet Sage. This plant is not easily hidden or tucked away in the garden. Flowers grow on long spikes and bloom from early summer until the frosts. There are also pink, white, and purple flowers. Plants grow from 1'-3' high and there are some dwarf varieties. In mild climates, plants often survive the winter and bloom again the following year.

Planting
- Young plants are sold at nurseries in spring.
- Plants prefer full sun, but will tolerate partial shade.
- Not particular about soil. Plant 12"-18" apart.
- Because most of the flowers are so vivid, it is best to plant in masses as they do not blend well with other plants.

Care
- Plants require lots of water.
- Feed occasionally with a well-balanced fertilizer.
- Plants readily reseed themselves. In mild climates, young plants often pop up in spring. These can be transplanted.
- Flowers do not last well when cut.

SHASTA DAISY

Chrysanthemum maximum

Shasta daisies are sturdy perennials and grow in almost all climates. Plants are 2'-4' high and dwarfs are 1' high. In olden days, flowers were single. Now there are single, double, semi-double, fluffy, frilly, and shaggy. Most all are white with yellow centers, but there are some light yellow ones. They bloom in summer and fall. Plants are fast growers, and the flowers are superb for cutting.

Daisies are often dyed another color, particularly on St. Patrick's Day when a lot of green ones suddenly appear. This is another typical example of defacing nature.

Planting
- Young plants are available in spring and fall at nurseries. They are also easily grown from seeds.
- Plant in full sun, but in hot climates in partial shade.
- Space plants 1' apart as they rapidly grow into a small clump.
- Not particular about soil, but will do best in a fairly rich one with good drainage.

Care
- Plants like lots of water and often wilt on hot days, but they perk up in the cool of the evening.
- Cut off faded flowers. This is called "deadheading".
- Every two or three years, divide crowded clumps in spring. In mild climates, this can also be done in fall.

Shasta Daisies are a boon

to gardeners who do not

have green thumbs.

Plants practically grow

by themselves.

SNAPDRAGON

Antirrhinum majus

Snapdragons are just as enchanting as their name. They are perennials, but are usually treated as annuals, and they grow to various heights. Tall ones are 2'-3' high, intermediates 18", and dwarfs 6"-9" high. The tall and intermediate varieties look majestic against a wall or fence or as a background in borders. Dwarf ones make colorful borders.

Flowers are single or double and have many combinations of gorgeous shades of deep red, rose, crimson, yellow, apricot, and white. They bloom in spring and early summer, and in mild and hot climates, in winter and spring. There are some strains with flowers that do not have snapping jaws.

Planting

- In mild climates, plant young plants in early fall. In cold climates, in early spring after frosts. Plants should be from rust resistant strains.
- Plant in full sun, but will tolerate partial shade.
- Plant in a rich soil. Space tall varieties 18"-2' apart and others 8"-12" apart.

Care

- Pinch back center stem when plants are about 6" high for a bushy plant and more blooms. Do not pinch tall varieties if you want a stately plant.
- Feed regularly with a well-balanced fertilizer, and stake the tall varieties.
- In mild climates when flowers fade, cut plants back to 6"-8" and feed with a fish emulsion. Plants might bloom again.
- Never water overhead. Plants are susceptible to rust and this encourages it. Also to further prevent rust, do not plant snapdragons in the same spot as the year before.

The name of this beautiful

flower fascinates me.

Whenever I hear it, I think

of mysterious China,

opium dens, and exquisite,

satin robes with swirling

dragons embroidered with

the forbidden stitch.

SNOWFLAKE, SUMMER SNOWFLAKE & SNOWDROP

Leucojum aestivum & Galanthus nivalis

A Lily-of-the-Valley

look-alike

Snowflakes are hardy bulbs. Flowers are larger and not nearly as fragrant as lily-of-the-valley, but they are similar and a good substitute for them in bouquets. Plants require very little care and will grow in most areas. They multiply rapidly and can be left in the ground undisturbed for years. Most gardeners naturalize them under trees and shrubs.

The white, slightly scented flowers have a touch of green on their tips. They are bell-shaped on 18" stems with two or more blooms per stem. The leaves resemble slender swords. In warm climates, they bloom in late fall through winter, and in other climates in early spring.

Snowdrops (*Galanthus*) are often confused with snowflakes. They are both bulbs and both have the same care, but snowdrops prefer cold climates. The flowers are bulbular and there is only one bloom per stem. Plants prefer a rich, moist soil.

Planting
- Plant in fall in sun or partial shade.
- Plant 4" deep and 3" apart.
- Not particular about soil.

Care
- Feed with a high-bloom fertilizer (2-10-10) when foliage is about 6" high.
- Do not disturb plants unless clumps begin to bulge. Then divide after the blooming period and after foliage has died.

STATICE, SEA LAVENDER, EVERLASTING FLOWER
Limonium perezii

Statice is a perennial that grows in clumps about a foot high with clusters of flowers on stems up to 3' high. Plants are more a small shrub than a bedding plant. They are good for background planting, along fences and driveways, and are often used as a fire retardant in dry areas. Plants thrive near the seashore and can withstand salty wind, salty soil, and hot sun. The clusters of small dainty flowers are a deep lavender with tiny white centers. There are also some varieties with white, yellow, or pink flowers. In mild climates they bloom from June all through summer. In colder climates summer bloom is shorter. Flowers are great for cutting and excellent for drying. They are affectionately called the everlasting flower.

Planting
- Plants are available at nurseries in gallon cans in spring. Old plants can also be divided for new ones.
- Plant in full sun in a soil with good drainage.
- Statice often self-sows and seedlings pop up in unexpected places - like vacant lots.

By the sea, by the sea,

by the beautiful sea

Care
- Requires little or no care.
- Feed occasionally with a balanced fertilizer and do not overwater.

STOCK

Matthiola incana

Kubla Khan's Xanadu

Stock has a spicy fragrance that is difficult to describe, but it is very exotic. Last spring, I had a large bowl of long-stemmed, white stock on my coffee table. The scent was overwhelming. I closed my eyes and envisioned I was in one of the courtyards of the Moorish Alhambra in Spain. I could hear water splashing from the hundreds of fountains, and sounds of laughter and gaiety from the rooms of the harem.

Maybe I wasn't in Spain at all, but in Kubla Khan's Xanadu, "and there were gardens bright with sinuous rills where blossomed many an incense bearing tree." (Samuel Coleridge)

Wherever I was, the smell of stock was intoxicating.

Stock is a perennial, but plants are treated as annuals. They will tolerate frosts that aren't too severe. Flowers are single or double and there are many shades of pink, purple, cream, and white. Column stock and Double Giant Flowering varieties have long stems and regal, full blooms. They are the darlings of florists. Plants of the Giant Imperial strain are branched and grow about 2' high. The quick maturing Trysomic strains are best where summers are hot.

STOCK

Planting

- In mild climates plant in fall for winter and spring bloom. In cold climates, plant in early spring for spring bloom.
- Plant in full sun. In hot areas, in partial shade.
- Plant in a light, rich soil with good drainage.
- Plant tall strains 10" apart, and smaller strains 6"-8" apart.

Care

- For a bushier plant and more flowers, pinch back plants when they are 6"-10". Do not pinch back the tall strains if you want long-stemmed flowers for cutting.
- Feed regularly with a balanced fertilizer until buds form.
- Keep plants well watered but be sure they have good drainage as they are subject to root rot.
- Few pests bother stock.

SUNFLOWER, COMMON SUNFLOWER
Helianthus annuus

Faces Pointing Towards the Sun

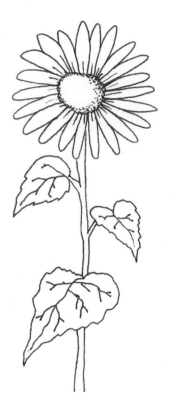

The rain in Spain might lie mainly on the plain, but hundreds of fields planted with rows of large, bobbing sunflowers also lie on Spanish plains. These plants, whose faces point toward the scorching sun, add a colorful touch to the countryside, and they are a wonderful contrast to the groves of old, gnarled olive and cork trees. Sunflower seeds have become an important crop in Spain.

Some sunflowers are perennials, but this one is an annual. Plants are very hardy and thrive in the heat and sun. They are extremely fast growing and bloom in August and early fall.

There are some ornamental varieties, but to me, there is only one sunflower, and that is the tall, old-fashioned common sunflower. They make a garden look like Kansas in August. These giants add a whimsical, earthy touch of warmth and cheeriness to a spot along a fence or wall.

Planting
- In spring, sow seeds directly in the ground in any type of soil with good drainage. Ornamental types like a slightly rich soil.
- Sow seeds in full sun 1/2" deep and 1' apart. They will sprout in five days.

Care
- Plants need very little care, but if they are fed every two weeks with a well-balanced fertilizer and given lots of water, they will be spectacular.
- When seedlings are about a foot high, make a 6" high mound of soil around the stems to give support for the heavy flowers.
- Stake plants if necessary.

SWEET PEA

Lathyrus odoratus

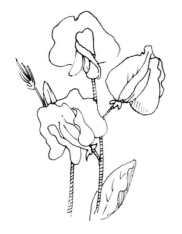

A Dreadful Event

When I was in the Second Grade, my teacher decided the class should give a play, and each child would represent a flower. I was a sweet pea and wore a dress and hat which were completely covered with pale, pink, ruffled, organdy petals. Even my mother didn't recognize me! Fortunately, this dreadful event didn't turn me against this graceful and prolific flower.

Sweet peas are annuals, and in mild climates different varieties bloom from December through spring. In colder climates they bloom in spring and summer. The most popular varieties are the climbing ones that grow 6'-8' high with flowers that are excellent for cutting. There are also bush varieties that grow 1'-2' high. They are used as borders, massed in beds, and planted in containers.

All sweet peas like cool weather and cannot tolerate heat unless they are a heat-resistant variety. The name Cuthbertson on a package of seeds indicates they can resist heat, but in hot climates even these will not thrive.

Flowers have a subtle fragrance and are soft shades of pink, salmon, blue, lavender, and cream. Others are deep red, rose, purple, and white, and some are a mixture of a single color on either a white or cream background. There are early flowering, spring flowering, and summer flowering vine varieties.

SWEET PEA

Planting
- Sweet peas are usually grown from seeds that are sown directly in the ground. Small plants are also available at some nurseries.
- In mild climates, plant Early Flowering ones in August or early September, Spring Flowering ones from October to early January, and Summer Flowering ones in late spring. In colder climates, plant Spring Flowering types in early spring after the frosts, and Summer Flowering ones in late spring.
- Plant in a sunny spot with good air circulation.
- Soak seeds in water for several hours before planting. This speeds up the sprouting as seeds are slow to germinate.
- Dig a trench about 14" deep and 6" wide. Mix some peat moss and ground bark with the soil and refill trench to within 1 1/2" of the top. Water and let settle for at least two hours. Sow seeds 2" apart and cover with 2" of soil.
- Put a trellis alongside covered trench and put out snail bait. If planted near a wall or fence, place trellis at least 6" away for good air circulation. Plants are susceptible to mildew.
- Bush type plants do not need a trench. Sow seeds in flats and transplant them 12" apart.

Care
- When seedlings are about 6" high, pinch tops to make fuller plants.
- Sweet peas like lots of water. Always deep water plants.
- Feed at least once a month with a balanced fertilizer.
- Pick flowers as often as possible. The more you pick, the more you get. Do not let seed pods develop as this slows down the development of flowers. If you want to save seeds for the following year, let pods develop at end of season.

SWEET WILLIAM

Dianthus barbatus

A Misnomer

The name of this plant is as deceiving as the promises of a politician and as phony as King Kong. There isn't anything sweet about Sweet William. It is a very sturdy, dependable biennial, which is often treated as an annual, and is one of the oldest flowers to be grown in gardens. It was a great favorite of Henry VIII at Hampton Court.

The low, bushy plants have stems 8"-20" high. There are dwarf varieties 4"-10" high. Plants of the Wee Willie strain (4" high) are very popular. Flowers are single or double and grow in clusters of brilliant pink, deep red, violet, white, and many are bi-colored. They bloom in spring and summer and are excellent for borders and color spots in beds.

Planting
- In mild climates, plant young plants in spring or fall. In cold climates, in early spring after the frosts.
- Plant in full sun 10"-12" apart in a fairly rich soil with good drainage.
- If plant is in the right location, it often reseeds itself.

Care
- Do not overwater.
- Fertilize regularly with a balanced fertilizer.

TIGER FLOWER, MEXICAN SHELL FLOWER

Tigridia pavonia

Tiger flowers are bulbs and are members of the iris family. They are native to Mexico and have leaves shaped like swords. Each flower on 1'-2' stems blooms for one day and dies, but there are many others to replace it. The beautiful, shell-like flowers bloom in July and August and are splashy shades of red, orange, yellow, or white with dark, splotchy markings in the centers.

Planting

- Plant in mid-spring in full sun, or partial shade in hot areas.
- Plant bulbs 3" deep and 4"-8" apart in a rich, sandy soil with good drainage. They are spectacular when planted in groups of eight or more.
- An excellent container plant.

Care

- Keep well-watered during growing season.
- Feed every two weeks with a fish emulsion.
- Watch for gophers. They love to eat the bulbs.
- In warm climates keep bulbs in ground and divide clumps every three or four years after blooming period.
- In cold climates dig up bulbs when foliage turns yellow and store in sand, peat moss, or sawdust in a dry, cool spot. If clumps need dividing, do this the following spring just before planting.

"Tiger! Tiger!

burning bright

In the forests of the night,

What immortal hand

or eye Could frame thy

fearful symmetry?"

William Blake

TUBEROSE

Polianthes tuberosa

Plants have tuberous roots and swordlike leaves that resemble tall grass. Some varieties have variegated foliage. The waxen, white flowers grow in small clusters on 2'-3' stems, and they bloom in early summer until fall. Flowers are single and double. Tuberoses are good bedding or container plants, and flowers are excellent for cutting.

Planting

- In cold climates, plant in spring when ground gets warm. In warm climates, can be planted anytime from January to March. Tubers should have some green showing at the stem end, and they can be started in peat or sphagnum moss before planting.
- Plant in a well protected, but warm spot in the sun, or in partial shade in warm climates.
- Plant 1"-2" deep and 4"-6" apart in a rich soil with good drainage.

Care

- Water lightly until shoots appear, then keep well watered during growing period, but do not let soil get soggy.
- Feed regularly with a balanced fertilizer.
- In cold climates, after blooming, dig up tubers when leaves turn yellow. Store in a dry cool place in sand or peat moss. Oftentimes they do not bloom the second year.
- In warm climates, leave tubers in ground and divide clumps every 3 or 4 years.

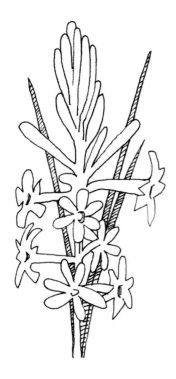

There is no need to wear

Chanel No. 5 or English

Leather After Shave - as

the case may be - when a

few sprays of tuberoses are

in the house. Their exotic

fragrance is overwhelming.

TUBEROUS BEGONIA

Begonia tuberhybrida

Tuberous begonias like fairly cool summers and moist air, and thrive along the coast of California. In hot climates it is necessary to have nursemaids around the clock to constantly mist them. Plants are easy to grow if they are in the right climate.

There are many varieties of these begonias. Some grow 12"-18" high and others are great in hanging baskets. They do not make good house plants as they need fresh air circulating around them. There is a new strain that has been developed called 'Non-Stop', and flowers have a very long blooming season.

Flowers bloom all summer and into fall. They are single, semi-double, double, ruffled, frilled, double ruffled, and double frilled. There are unbelievably beautiful shades of oranges, pinks, reds, yellows, and white. Some have a contrasting color on the tips of their petals, and others have fringed petals. All are spectacular.

Alexander the Great,

Peter the Great,

Catherine the Great, and

Tuberous Begonia!

All are Great!

Planting

- Start begonias in March from tubers. These are available at nurseries or can be ordered from growers.
- Plants must be grown in shade and semi-shade and will only tolerate morning sun. Plant in a sheltered place out of the wind.
- Tubers are often started in slightly moist peat moss, sphagnum moss, or vermiculite. Keep them out of the direct sun and keep them moist but not soggy. When tubers have two leaves, transplant into pots or into the ground.

TUBEROUS BEGONIA

- Tubers can also be planted directly in pots or in the ground. They must have good drainage. When planting in pots, add redwood shavings to a light, prepared planter mix. When planting in the ground, put about 8" of redwood shavings on top of soil and either work the shavings in the soil or plant tubers directly in them. Plant 1" deep.

Care

- When sprouts are about 2" high, fertilize with 1/2 strength fish emulsion. When plants are established, fertilize twice a month with full strength.
- Stake plants before the delicate stems break. Sometimes four stakes per plant are necessary.
- Do not overwater as plants are subject to root rot.
- If young flowers drop off before fully opening, it is probably due either to overwatering or overfeeding.
- Plants are subject to mildew. Spray with benomyl.
- When plants stop blooming in late fall, let them die back and water very sparingly. When leaves wither and die, stop watering.

Ways to Store Tubers in Winter

- Leave them in their pots and store pots on their side in a cool, dry place.
- Take tubers from pots with a clump of soil, and put in a cool, dry place. When tubers are completely dormant and soil is dry, they can be stored without the soil in dry peat moss or vermiculite.
- In warm climates, they can be left in the ground, but this is risky.
- In March when pink sprouts appear, plant tubers once again in a carefully prepared soil and cross your fingers. Sometimes they sprout, and sometimes they don't.

TULIP

Tulipa

All tulips are bulbs that thrive in climates with cold winters. They can also be successfully grown in warm climates if they are refrigerated for 6-8 weeks before planting. The best bulbs come from the land of windmills and dikes. There are early and late blooming tulips. Some are tall and some are short. Flowers are single, double, striped, ruffled and fringed. The colors of the flowers are limitless. There are solid colored, variegated, and striped varieties.

Planting

- In cold climates, plant bulbs in October, or any time after the ground cools and before it freezes. In warm climates, keep bulbs in an open paper sack in the lower part of the refrigerator for at least 6-8 weeks before planting in December or January. Small bulbs are no bargains. They probably won't bloom. The best size to buy is one that is at least 5" wide.
- Tulips are sun worshippers. In cold climates, plant in full sun, and in warm climates, they can also be planted in partial shade.
- Plant in a rich soil with good drainage. Put the pointed end of the bulb up.
- Some experts say to plant tulips 2 1/2 times as deep as the width of the bulb and about 6" apart. The Wise Old Owl in the Ginkgo Tree plants his bulbs 10" deep. He believes bulbs will have cooler roots and stronger foliage and flowers if planted a little deeper than normal.

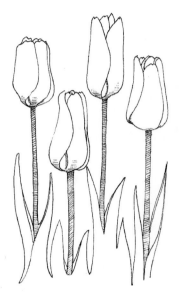

Tip toe,

through the tulips

TULIP

Care

- Feed with a balanced fertilizer when leaves first appear.
- Keep plants well watered.
- In cold climates, bulbs can be left in the ground. Mulch them with a thick layer of rotted cow manure when the ground freezes.
- In warm climates, it is best to dig them up and store in a cool, dry spot for the summer. If they are kept in a temperature of 78 degrees or more, they will probably not bloom the next year. Most gardeners throw out their tulip bulbs because blooms are not as large the second year - if they bloom at all.

Things My Mother Never Told Me

- If rodents are a nuisance, protect bulbs with a wire mesh - or bury a moth ball or moth crystals with each bulb.
- Tulips are more effective if planted in groups of the same variety and same color.
- When planting lots of tulips, dig a trench or a large hole rather than individual holes.

If the rose is queen of the garden, the tulip is king.

The majestic, regal flowers give class to a garden.

VERBENA

Verbena hybrida

Verbenas are fast spreading plants that satisfy the impatient gardener who wants "instant" results. They are perennials, but in cold climates are treated as annuals. Plants grow 6"-12" high and are used in beds and containers, as ground covers, along driveways, or cascading over walls. The many-branched plants are low growing and have profuse, flat clusters of flowers that bloom from June to late fall. Colors are blue, lavender, pink, salmon, scarlet, red and white. They love hot climates and can withstand droughts.

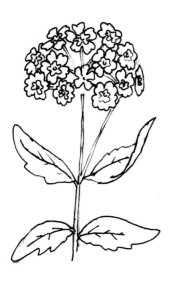

Verbenas are the

A. J. Foyts and

Jesse Owenses

of the garden.

Planting
- Bedding plants are available at nurseries in spring. Cuttings can also be made at this time. See Chapter Fourteen, "How to Beat Inflation by Propagation."
- Plant in full sun in an average soil.
- Plants grow so rapidly they can be placed 2' apart for a ground cover. For other purposes, place 8"-12" apart.

Care
- Keep on the dry side. Water deeply and not too often.
- In mild climates, cut back plants drastically in late winter or early spring.
- In cold climates, cover plants with a fairly heavy mulch and plants might survive if winters are not too cold.

VERONICA, SPEEDWELL
Veronica hybrids

A Stray, Mongrel Puppy

When my daughter was in High School, she brought home a stray, mongrel puppy. We named her Veronica because we wanted a glamorous name to counteract her ordinary background. Veronica, the plant, could have been given this name for the same reason. The flowers are attractive, but they aren't quite as sophisticated as many other flowers in the garden. However, veronicas are one of the most reliable, easy-to-grow, and prolific plants in the garden.

This species of veronica is a compact, bushy plant and a hardy perennial. Spikes of "true blue" flowers are on stems 1'-2' high. Other colors are rose, deep pink and white. Flowers are long-lasting and bloom in the summer.

Planting
- Plant young plants in spring. Plants can also be divided at this time.
- Plant 1'-2' apart in average soil in full sun, or partial shade in warm climates.
- The flowers brighten up borders and rock gardens.

Care
- Plants need little or no care. They are very accommodating.
- Occasionally feed with a balanced fertilizer.
- Cut off spikes after they have bloomed.
- Divide clumps in spring if necessary.

174

VIOLA, TUFTED PANSY
Viola cornuta

Violas are first cousins of pansies. Their flowers are a solid color with yellow centers, and they have a slender spur. They are short-lived perennials, but are usually treated as annuals. Plants grow 6"-8" high and are excellent as borders, in containers, and hanging baskets. There are also some dwarf varieties 2" high. In most areas flowers bloom from early spring to late fall. In mild climates they bloom almost year round. There are many beautiful shades of violet, yellow, blue, apricot, and deep red and white.

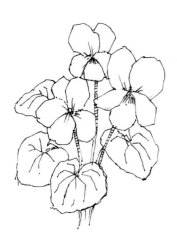

At the "fin de siècle",

many girls were named

after flowers such as Viola,

Rose, Myrtle, Iris, Olive,

and Violet.

Planting
- In mild climates, plant in fall for winter and spring color, and in spring for summer and fall color. In cold climates, plant in spring. Buy young plants that are just starting to branch.
- Plant in full sun in coastal areas, and in partial shade in mild or hot climates.
- Plant in a rich soil for best results.

Care
- Keep well-watered and feed regularly with a well-balanced fertilizer.
- Keep dead flowers picked and pinch back plants when they get straggly.
- In mild climates, severely cut back plants in late fall.

VIOLET

Viola oderata

Violets are close relatives of violas and pansies, and they grow wild in many parts of the country. Plants are perennials and vary in size from 2"-8" high. They spread by runners and are extremely hardy and require little or no care. They make good ground covers, borders, or are effective naturalized under trees. The small, dainty flowers are fragrant, and are various shades of purple, rose, and white. In mild climates they bloom in winter and spring. In cold climates, in spring and summer.

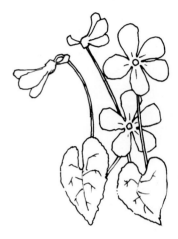

Planting
- In mild climates, plant or divide in late fall. In cold climates, in spring.
- In cool areas, plant in sun or partial shade. In mild climates, in partial shade. In hot climates, in full shade. Plants are often naturalized under trees.
- Not particular about soil, but plants do best in a fairly rich one.

Care
- Feed with a balanced fertilizer in early spring when plants begin to get new growth.
- Keep well-watered and watch for spider mites. They often appear in midsummer.
- In late fall cut back straggly plants. This will produce better blooms the following season.
- Divide clumps about every two or three years.

"Your scent will bring

back to us

Long vanished hours"

From the Marlborough

School song

YARROW, MILFOIL
Achillea millefolium

In many areas yarrows have become naturalized and are considered lowly weeds by the haughty intelligentsia, who greatly malign a very charming plant. The perennial plants flourish in gardens and flowers bloom over a long period during summer and fall. Flowers are yellow, white, and different shades of red, and they grow in flat-topped clusters on stems that are sometimes 3' long. They are excellent for flower arrangements. Some varieties help retard fires.

Planting
- In mild climates, plant in fall or early spring. In colder climates, in spring after the frosts.
- Plant in full sun 12"-18" apart in a soil that isn't too rich.

Care
- Do not overwater. Plants can tolerate dry soil.
- Cut plants back after flowers have bloomed.
- Divide about every three years when clumps get crowded.

Yarrow grows in almost every part of the world except the North and South Poles.

ZINNIA

Zinnia elegans

Zinnias are annuals that bloom in summer and early fall. They are sun worshippers and love hot weather. However, the most gorgeous and largest zinnias I have ever seen were in Gig Harbor, Washington, which isn't exactly the Gobi Desert, and they didn't have a trace of mildew.

There are many varieties of zinnias. Height of plants are Tall (2'-3' high), Medium (1'-2'), Dwarf (12"), and Extra Dwarf (6"). All varieties have flowers in various vibrant shades of pink, orange, yellow, purple, white and green. Some are bi-colored. There are single, double, and cushioned centers. Others are shaggy and some have quilled rays.

Planting

- Do not plant until weather gets really warm as they will not grow until it does. June or July are good months for planting.
- Plant in full sun in a rich soil.
- Plant tall ones 1' apart. Medium ones 8"-10" apart, and dwarfs 6"-8" apart.

Planting

- If you want plants to be bushy with more blooms, pinch them back when they are about 6" high.
- Feed with a balanced fertilizer at least twice before they bloom.
- Keep well-watered but do not let soil get soggy. Never water overhead as plants are prone to mildew. If they do get this disease, spray with benomyl.
- Remove plants from garden when they get straggly.

Zinnias are vibrant flowers that add a "zing" to a summer garden.

EPILOGUE

Charles Barr, an eminent

horticulturist, says,

"The best way to get enjoyment out of

gardening is to put on an old hat,

dress in old clothes, hold a trowel in

one hand and a cool drink in the other,

and tell the man where to dig."